DEPARTMENT OF THE TREASURY
TECHNICAL EXPLANATION OF THE CONVENTION BETWEEN
THE GOVERNMENT OF THE UNITED STATES OF AMERICA
AND
THE GOVERNMENT OF THE KINGDOM OF THAILAND
FOR THE AVOIDANCE OF DOUBLE TAXATION
AND THE PREVENTION OF FISCAL EVASION
WITH RESPECT TO TAXES ON INCOME
SIGNED AT BANGKOK ON NOVEMBER 26, 1996

DEPARTMENT OF THE TREASURY
TECHNICAL EXPLANATION OF THE CONVENTION BETWEEN
THE GOVERNMENT OF THE UNITED STATES OF AMERICA
AND
THE GOVERNMENT OF THE KINGDOM OF THAILAND
FOR THE AVOIDANCE OF DOUBLE TAXATION
AND THE PREVENTION OF FISCAL EVASION
WITH RESPECT TO TAXES ON INCOME
SIGNED AT BANGKOK ON NOVEMBER 26, 1996

INTRODUCTION

This document is a technical explanation of the Convention between the United States and Thailand which was signed on November 26, 1996 (the "Convention"). References in this Explanation to the "U.S. Model" are to the United States Model Income Tax Convention, published on September 30, 1996. The U.S. Model was published following negotiation of the Convention, but the Convention reflects substantial consistency with the language and policies of the U.S. Model. References to the "OECD Model" are to the Model Tax Convention on Income and on Capital, published by the OECD in 1992, as subsequently amended. References to the "U.N. Model" are to the United Nations Model Double Taxation Convention between Developed and Developing Countries, published in 1980.

The Technical Explanation is an official guide to the Convention. It reflects the policies behind particular Convention provisions, as well as understandings reached with respect to the application and interpretation of the Convention.

Article 1 (Personal Scope)

Paragraph 1

Paragraph 1 of Article 1 provides that the Convention applies to residents of the United States or Thailand, except where the terms of the Convention provide otherwise. Under Article 4 (Residence) a person is generally treated as a resident of a Contracting State if that person is, under the laws of that State, liable to tax therein by reason of his domicile or other similar criteria. If, however, a person is considered a resident of both Contracting States, a single state of residence is assigned under Article 4. This definition governs for all purposes of the Convention.

Certain provisions are applicable to persons who may not be residents of either Contracting State. For example, Article 21 (Government Service) may apply to an employee of a Contracting State who is resident in neither State. Paragraph 1 of Article 26 (Non-Discrimination) applies to nationals of the Contracting States. Under Article 28 (Exchange of Information), information may be exchanged with respect to residents of third states.

Paragraph 2

Paragraph 2 contains the traditional saving clause found in all U.S. treaties. The Contracting States reserve their rights, except as provided in paragraph 3, to tax their residents and citizens as provided in their internal laws, notwithstanding any provisions of the Convention to the contrary. For example, if a resident of Thailand is present in the United States for less than 90 days to perform independent personal services, the income from the services is not attributable to a fixed base in the United States, and he receives less than $10,000 in remuneration, Article 15 (Independent Personal Services) would normally prevent the United States from taxing the income. If, however, the resident of Thailand is also a citizen of the United States, the saving clause permits the United States to include the remuneration in the worldwide income of the citizen and subject it to tax under the normal U.S. Internal Revenue Code (the "Code") rules (*i.e.*, without regard to Code section 894(a)).

For purposes of the saving clause, "residence" is determined under Article 4 (Residence). Thus, if an individual who is not a U.S. citizen is a resident of the United States under the Code, and is also a resident of Thailand under its law, and that individual has a permanent home available to him in Thailand and not in the United States, he would be treated as a resident of Thailand under Article 4 and for purposes of the saving clause. The United States would not be permitted to apply its statutory rules to that person if they are inconsistent with the treaty. Thus, an individual who is a U.S. resident under the Code but who is deemed to be a resident of Thailand under the tie-breaker rules of Article 4 (Residence) would be subject to U.S. tax only to the extent permitted by the Convention. However, the person would be treated as a U.S. resident for U.S. tax purposes other than determining the individual's U.S. tax liability. For example, in determining under Code section 957 whether a foreign corporation is a controlled foreign corporation, shares in that corporation held by the individual would be considered to be held by a U.S. resident. As a result, other U.S. citizens or residents might be deemed to be United States shareholders of a controlled foreign corporation subject to current inclusion of Subpart F income recognized by the corporation. See, Treas. Reg. section 301.7701(b)-7(a)(3).

Under paragraph 2 each Contracting State also reserves its right to tax former citizens whose loss of citizenship had as one of its principal purposes the avoidance of tax. This right extends only for a period of 10 years following such loss. The United States also reserves its right to tax former long-term lawful residents whose loss of residence status had as one of its principal purposes the avoidance of tax as though the Convention had not come into force (whether or not such person is determined to be a U.S. resident under Article 4 (Residence)). This right, also, extends only for a period of 10 years following the loss of residence.

For purposes of these "expatriation" rules, the United States treats an individual as having a principal purpose to avoid tax if (a) the average annual net income tax of such individual for the period of 5 taxable years ending before the date of the loss of status is greater than $100,000, or (b) the net worth of such individual as of such date is $500,000 or more. The United States defines "long-term resident" as an individual (other than a U.S. citizen) who is a lawful permanent resident of the United States in at least 8 of the prior 15 taxable years. An individual shall not be treated as a lawful permanent resident for any taxable year if such individual is treated as a resident of a foreign country under the provisions of a tax treaty between the United States and the foreign country and the individual does not waive the benefits of such treaty applicable to residents of the foreign country. Such a former citizen or long-term resident is taxable in the United States in accordance with the provisions of section 877 of the Code.

Paragraph 3

Some provisions of the Convention are intended to provide benefits by a Contracting State to its citizens and residents that do not exist under its internal law. Paragraph 3 sets forth certain exceptions to the saving clause that preserve these benefits for citizens and residents of the Contracting States. Subparagraph (a) lists certain provisions of the Convention that are applicable to all citizens and residents of a Contracting State, despite the general saving clause rule of paragraph 2: (1) Paragraph 2 of Article 9 (Associated Enterprises) grants the right to a correlative adjustment with respect to income tax due on profits reallocated under Article 9. (2) Paragraphs 2 and 5 of Article 20 (Pensions and Social Security Payments) deal with social security benefits and child support payments, respectively. The inclusion of paragraph 2 in the exceptions to the saving clause means that the grant of exclusive taxing right of social security benefits to the paying country applies to deny, for example, to the United States the right to tax its citizens and residents on social security benefits paid by Thailand. The inclusion of paragraph 5, which exempts child support payments from taxation by the State of residence of the recipient, means that if a resident of Thailand pays child support to a citizen or resident of the United States, the United States may not tax the recipient. (3) Article 25 (Relief from Double Taxation) confirms the benefit of a credit to citizens and residents of one Contracting State for income taxes paid to the other. (4) Article 26 (Non-Discrimination) requires one Contracting State to grant national treatment to residents and citizens of the other Contracting State in certain circumstances. Excepting this Article from the saving clause requires, for example, that the United States give such benefits to a resident or citizen of Thailand even if that person is a citizen of the United States. (5) Article 27 (Mutual Agreement Procedure) may confer benefits by a Contracting State on its citizens and residents. For example, the statute of limitations may be waived for refunds and the competent authorities are permitted to use a definition of a term that differs from the internal law definition. These benefits are intended to be granted by a Contracting State to its citizens and residents.

Subparagraph (b) of paragraph 3 provides a different set of exceptions to the saving clause. The benefits referred to are all intended to be granted to temporary residents of a Contracting State (for example, in the case of the United States, holders of non-immigrant visas), but not to citizens or to persons who have acquired permanent residence in that State. If beneficiaries of these provisions travel from one of the Contracting States to the other, and remain in the other long enough to become residents under its internal law, but do not acquire permanent residence status (i.e., in the U.S. context, they do not become "green card" holders) and are not citizens of that State, the host State will continue to grant these benefits even if they conflict with the statutory rules. The benefits preserved by this paragraph are the host country exemptions for the following items of income: government service salaries and pensions under Article 21 (Government Service); certain income of visiting students and trainees under Article 22 (Students and Trainees); certain income of visiting teachers or researchers under Article 23 (Teachers); and the income of diplomatic agents and consular officers under Article 29 (Diplomatic Agents and Consular Officers).

Paragraph 4

Paragraph 4 states the generally accepted relationship both between the Convention and domestic law and between the Convention and other agreements between the Contracting States (i.e., that no provision in the Convention may restrict any exclusion, exemption, deduction, credit or other benefit accorded by the tax laws of the Contracting States, or by any other agreement between the Contracting States). For example, if a deduction would be allowed under the Code in computing the U.S. taxable income of a resident of Thailand, the deduction also is allowed to that person in computing taxable income under the Convention. Paragraph 4 also means that the Convention may not increase the tax burden on a resident of a Contracting State beyond the burden determined under domestic law. Thus, a right to tax given by the Convention cannot be exercised unless that right also exists under internal law. The relationship between the non-discrimination provisions of the Convention and other agreements is not addressed in paragraph 4 but in paragraph 5.

It follows that under the principle of paragraph 4 a taxpayer's liability for U.S. tax need not be determined under the Convention if the Code would produce a more favorable result. A taxpayer may not, however, choose among the provisions of the Code and the Convention in an inconsistent manner in order to minimize tax. For example, assume that a resident of Thailand has three separate businesses in the United States. One is a profitable permanent establishment and the other two are trades or businesses that would earn taxable income under the Code but that do not meet the permanent establishment threshold tests of the Convention. One is profitable and the other incurs a loss. Under the Convention, the income of the permanent establishment is taxable, and both the profit and loss of the other two businesses are ignored. Under the Code, all three would be subject to tax, but the loss would be offset against the profits of the two profitable ventures. The taxpayer may not invoke the Convention to exclude the profits of the profitable trade or business and invoke the Code to claim the loss of the loss trade or business against the profit of the permanent establishment. (See Rev. Rul. 84-17, 1984-1 C.B. 308.) If, however, the taxpayer invokes the Code for the taxation of all three ventures, he would not be precluded from invoking the Convention with respect, for example, to any dividend income he may receive from the United States that is not effectively connected with any of his business activities in the United States.

Similarly, nothing in the Convention can be used to deny any benefit granted by any other agreement between the United States and Thailand. For example, if there were a Status of Forces Agreement between the United States and Thailand that provides certain benefits for military personnel or military contractors, those benefits or protections will be available to residents of the Contracting States regardless of any provisions to the contrary (or silence) in the Convention.

Paragraph 5

Paragraph 5 specifically relates to non-discrimination obligations of the Contracting States under other agreements. The provisions of paragraph 5 are an exception to the rule provided in paragraph 4 of this Article under which the Convention shall not restrict in any manner any benefit now or hereafter accorded by any other agreement between the Contracting States.

Subparagraph (a) of paragraph 5 provides that, notwithstanding any other agreement to which the Contracting States may be parties, a dispute concerning whether a measure is within the scope of this Convention shall be considered only by the competent authorities of the Contracting States, and the procedures under this Convention exclusively shall apply to the dispute. Thus, procedures for dealing with disputes that may be incorporated into trade, investment, or other agreements between the Contracting States shall not apply for the purpose of determining the scope of the Convention.

Subparagraph (b) of paragraph 5 provides that, unless the competent authorities determine that a taxation measure is not within the scope of this Convention, the nondiscrimination obligations of this Convention exclusively shall apply with respect to that measure, except for such national treatment or most-favored-nation ("MFN") obligations as may apply to trade in goods under the General Agreement on Tariffs and Trade ("GATT"). No national treatment or MFN obligation under any other agreement shall apply with respect to that measure. Thus, unless the competent authorities agree otherwise, any national treatment and MFN obligations undertaken by the Contracting States under agreements other than the Convention shall not apply to a taxation measure, with the exception of GATT as applicable to trade in goods.

Subparagraph (c) of paragraph 5 defines a "measure" broadly. It would include, for example, a law, regulation, rule, procedure, decision, administrative action or guidance, or any other form of measure.

Article 2 (Taxes Covered)

This Article specifies the U.S. taxes and the taxes of Thailand to which the Convention applies. Unlike Article 2 in the OECD Model, this Article does not contain a general description of the types of taxes that are covered (i.e., income taxes), but only a listing of the specific taxes covered for both of the Contracting States. With one exception, the taxes specified in Article 2 are the covered taxes for all purposes of the Convention. A broader coverage applies, however, for purposes of Article 28 (Exchange of Information). Article 28 applies with respect to all taxes imposed, in the case of the United States, under the Internal Revenue Code, and, in the case of Thailand, under the Revenue Code and under the Petroleum Tax Act.

Paragraph 1

Subparagraph 1(a) provides that the United States covered taxes are the Federal income taxes imposed by the Code. Although they may be regarded as income taxes, social security taxes (Code sections 1401, 3101, 3111 and 3301) are specifically excluded from coverage. It is expected that social security taxes will be dealt with in bilateral Social Security Totalization Agreements, which are negotiated and administered by the Social Security Administration. State and local taxes in the United States are not covered by the Convention. The U.S. taxes covered are referred to in the Convention as "United States tax."

In this Convention, like the U.S. Model, but unlike some U.S. treaties, the Accumulated Earnings Tax and the Personal Holding Companies Tax are covered taxes because they are income taxes and they are not otherwise excluded from coverage. Under the Code, these taxes will not apply to most foreign corporations because of a statutory exclusion or the corporation's failure to meet a statutory requirement. In the few cases where the taxes may apply to a foreign corporation, the tax due is likely to be insignificant. Treaty coverage therefore confers little if any benefit on such corporations.

Subparagraph 1(b) specifies the taxes of Thailand that are covered by the Convention are the income tax and the petroleum income tax. The Thai covered taxes are referred to in the Convention as "Thai tax."

Paragraph 2

Under paragraph 2, the Convention will apply to any taxes that are identical, or substantially similar, to those enumerated in paragraph 1, and which are imposed in addition to, or in place of, the existing taxes after the date of signature of the Convention.

The paragraph also provides that the competent authorities of the Contracting States will notify each other of significant changes in their taxation laws that affect their obligations under the Convention. The use of the term "significant" means that changes must be reported that are of significance to the operation of the Convention.

The competent authorities are also obligated to notify each other of official published materials concerning the application of the Convention. This requirement encompasses materials such as technical explanations, regulations, rulings and judicial decisions relating to the Convention.

Article 3 (General Definitions)

Paragraph 1

Paragraph 1 defines a number of basic terms used in the Convention. Certain others are defined in other articles of the Convention. For example, the term "resident of a Contracting State" is defined in Article 4 (Residence). The term "permanent establishment" is defined in Article 5 (Permanent Establishment). The terms "dividends," "interest" and "royalties" are defined in Articles 10, 11 and 12, respectively. The introduction to paragraph 1 makes clear that these definitions apply for all purposes of the Convention, unless the context requires otherwise. This latter condition allows flexibility in the interpretation of the treaty in order to avoid results not intended by the treaty's negotiators. Terms that are not defined in the Convention are dealt with in paragraph 2.

Subparagraph 1(a) defines the term "person" to include an individual, an estate, a trust, a partnership, a company and any other body of persons. The definition is significant for a variety of reasons. For example, under Article 4, only a "person" can be a "resident" and therefore eligible for most benefits under the treaty. Also, all "persons" are eligible to claim relief under Article 27 (Mutual Agreement Procedure).

This definition is more specific but not substantively different from the corresponding provision in the OECD Model. Unlike the OECD Model, it specifically includes a trust, an estate, and a partnership. Since, however, the OECD Model's definition also uses the phrase "and any other body of persons," partnerships would be included, consistent with paragraph 2 of the Article, to the extent that they are treated as "bodies of persons." Furthermore, because the OECD Model uses the term "includes," trusts and estates would be persons. Under Article 3(2) the meaning of the terms "partnership," "trust" and "estate" would be determined by reference to the law of the Contracting State whose tax is being applied.

The term "company" is defined in subparagraph 1(b) as a body corporate or an entity treated as a body corporate for tax purposes. In the case of the United States, the rules of Treas. Reg. section 301.7701-2 generally will apply to determine whether an entity is an association taxable as a corporation, and thus is a company, for purposes of the Convention. Similarly, in the case of the United States, a publicly traded partnership that is treated as a corporation under Code section 7704 will be treated as a company for purposes of the convention.

The terms "enterprise of a Contracting State" and "enterprise of the other Contracting State" are defined in subparagraph 1(c) as an enterprise carried on by a resident of a Contracting State and an enterprise carried on by a resident of the other Contracting State. The term "enterprise" is not defined in the Convention, nor is it defined in the OECD Model or its Commentaries. Despite the absence of a clear, generally accepted meaning for the term "enterprise," the term is understood to refer to any activity or set of activities that constitutes a trade or business. It is our understanding that the term encompasses an enterprise conducted through an entity (such as a partnership) that is treated as fiscally transparent in the Contracting State where the entity's owner is resident. Further, an enterprise conducted by such an entity will be treated as carried on by a resident of a Contracting State to the extent its partners or other owners are residents. This approach is consistent with the Code, which under section 875 attributes a trade or business conducted by a partnership to its partners and a trade or business conducted by an estate or trust to its beneficiaries.

An enterprise of a Contracting State need not be carried on in that State. It may be carried on in the other Contracting State or a third state (e.g., a U.S. corporation doing all of its business in Thailand would still be a U.S. enterprise).

Subparagraph 1(d) defines the term "international traffic." The term means any transport by a ship or aircraft except when the vessel is operated solely between places in the other Contracting State. This definition is applicable principally in the context of Article 8 (Shipping and Air Transport).

The exclusion from international traffic of transport solely between places in the other Contracting State means, for example, that carriage of goods or passengers solely between New York and Chicago by a Thai carrier (if this were possible under U.S. law) would not be treated as international traffic. The substantive taxing rules of the Convention relating to the taxation of income from transport, principally Article 8 (Shipping and Air Transport), therefore, would not apply to income from such carriage. The income would, however, be treated as business profits under Article 7 (Business Profits), and therefore would be taxable in the United States only if attributable to a U.S. permanent establishment of the Thai carrier, and then only on a net basis. The gross basis U.S. tax imposed by section 887 would not apply under the circumstances described. If, however, goods or passengers are carried by a carrier resident in Thailand from a non-U.S. port to, for example, New York, and some of the goods or passengers continue on to Chicago, the entire transport would be international traffic. This would be true if the international carrier transferred the goods at the U.S. port of entry from a ship to a land vehicle, from a ship to a lighter, or even if the overland portion of the trip in the United States was handled by an independent carrier under contract with the original international carrier, so long as both parts of the trip were reflected in original bills of lading. For this reason, the Convention refers, in the definition of "international traffic," to "such transport" being solely between places in the other Contracting State, while the OECD Model refers to the ship or aircraft being operated solely between such places. The Convention's language is intended to make clear that, as in the above example, even if the goods are carried on a different aircraft for the internal portion of the international voyage than is used for the overseas portion of the trip, the definition applies to that internal portion as well as the external portion.

Finally, a "cruise to nowhere," i.e., a cruise beginning and ending in a port in the same Contracting State with no stops in a foreign port, would not constitute international traffic.

Subparagraphs 1(e)(i) and (ii) define the term "competent authority" for the United States and Thailand, respectively. The U.S. competent authority is the Secretary of the Treasury or his delegate. The Secretary of the Treasury has delegated the competent authority function to the Commissioner of Internal Revenue, who in turn has delegated the authority to the Assistant Commissioner (International). With respect to interpretative issues, the Assistant Commissioner acts with the concurrence of the Associate Chief Counsel (International) of the Internal Revenue Service. The Thai competent authority is the Minister of Finance or his authorized representative.

The term "United States" is defined in subparagraph 1(f) to mean the United States of America, and, thus, is understood to include the states, the District of Columbia and the territorial sea of the United States. The term does not include Puerto Rico, the Virgin Islands, Guam or any other U.S. possession or territory. For certain purposes, the definition is extended to include any area outside the territorial sea of the United States over which the United exercises rights in accordance with international law and U.S. law with respect to natural resource exploration and exploitation of the seabed and its subsoil. This extension of the definition applies, however, only if the person, property or activity to which the Convention is being applied is connected with such natural resource exploration or exploitation. Thus, it would not include any activity involving the sea floor of an area over which the United States exercised rights for natural resource purposes if that activity was unrelated to the exploration and exploitation of natural resources.

Thailand is defined in subparagraph 1(g) to mean the Kingdom of Thailand, and, thus, is understood to include the territorial sea of Thailand. For certain purposes, the definition is extended to include any area adjacent to the territorial waters of Thailand over which Thailand exercises rights in accordance with international law and Thai law, with respect to natural resource exploration and exploitation of the seabed or its subsoil. This extension of the definition applies, however, only if the person, property or activity to which the Convention is being applied is connected with such natural resource exploration or exploitation. Thus, it would not include any activity involving the sea floor of an area over which Thailand exercised rights for natural resource purposes if that activity was unrelated to the exploration and exploitation of natural resources.

The terms "a Contracting State" and "the other Contracting State" are defined in subparagraph 1(h) to mean the United States or Thailand, depending on the context.

The term "tax" is defined in subparagraph 1(j) to mean United States tax and Thai tax, depending on the context. Those two terms, in turn, are defined in Article 2 (Taxes Covered) to refer to the U.S. and Thai taxes covered, respectively.

The term "nationals," as it relates both to the United States and to Thailand, is defined in subparagraph 1(j). This term is relevant for purposes of Articles 21 (Government Service) and 26 (Non-Discrimination). A national of a Contracting States is (1) an individual who is a citizen or national of that State, and (2) any legal person, partnership, association or any other entity deriving its status, as such, from the law in force in that State.

Paragraph 2 provides that in the application of the Convention, any term used but not defined in the Convention will have the meaning that it has under the law of the Contracting State whose tax is being applied, unless the context requires otherwise, or unless the competent authorities agree to a common meaning. If the term is defined under both the tax and non-tax laws of a Contracting State, the definition in the tax law is understood to take precedence over the definition in the non-tax laws. There also may be cases where the tax laws of a State contain multiple definitions of the same term. In such a case, the definition used for purposes of the particular provision at issue, if any, should be used. If, however, the meaning of a term cannot be readily determined under the law of a Contracting State, or if there is a conflict in meaning under the laws of the two States that creates difficulties in the application of the Convention, the competent authorities may, pursuant to Article 27 (Mutual Agreement Procedure), agree to a common meaning in order to prevent double taxation or to further any other purpose of the Convention. Likewise, if the definition of a term under either paragraph (1) of Article 3 or the tax law of a Contracting State would result in a circumstance unintended by the treaty negotiators or by the Contracting States, the competent authorities may agree to a common meaning of the term. This is a case where "the context" requires the use of a different definition. The common meaning agreed to need not conform to the meaning of the term under the laws of either Contracting State.

It is understood that the reference in paragraph 2 to the law of a Contracting State means the law in effect at the time the treaty is being applied, not the law as in effect at the time the treaty was signed. The use of an ambulatory definition, however, may lead to results that are at variance with the intentions of the negotiators and of the Contracting States when the treaty was negotiated and ratified. The reference in both paragraphs 1 and 2 to the "context otherwise requiring" a definition different from the treaty definition, in paragraph 1, or from the internal law definition of the Contracting State whose tax is being imposed, under paragraph 2, refers to a circumstance where the result intended by the Contracting States is different from the result that would obtain under either the paragraph 1 definition or the statutory definition. Thus, the context may require the use of a different definition. Flexibility in determining the appropriate definition to use is required.

Article 4 (Residence)

This Article sets forth rules for determining whether a person is a resident of a Contracting State for purposes of the Convention. As a general matter only residents of the Contracting States may claim the benefits of the Convention, although certain benefits apply to nationals of a Contracting State, whether or not the person is a resident. The treaty definition of residence is to be used only for purposes of the Convention. The fact that a person is determined to be a resident of a Contracting State under Article 4 does not necessarily entitle that person to the benefits of the Convention. In addition to being a resident, a person also must qualify for benefits under Article 18 (Limitation on Benefits) in order to receive benefits conferred on residents of a Contracting State.

The determination of residence for treaty purposes looks first to a person's liability to tax as a resident under the respective taxation laws of the Contracting States. As a general matter, a person who, under those laws, is a resident of one Contracting State and not of the other need look no further. That person is a resident for purposes of the Convention of the State in which he is resident under internal law. If, however, a person is resident in both Contracting States under their respective taxation laws, the Article proceeds, where possible, to assign a single State of residence to such a person for purposes of the Convention through the use of tie-breaker rules.

Paragraph 1

The term "resident of a Contracting State" is defined in paragraph 1. In general, this definition incorporates the definitions of residence in U.S. law and that of Thailand by referring to a resident as a person who, under the laws of a Contracting State, is subject to tax there by reason of his domicile, residence, citizenship, place of management, place of incorporation or any other similar criterion. Thus, residents of the United States include aliens who are considered U.S. residents under Code section 7701(b). The paragraph states that the term "resident of a Contracting State" also includes the Government of a Contracting State, as well as political subdivisions and local authorities.

Certain entities that are nominally subject to tax but that in practice rarely pay tax also would generally be treated as residents and therefore accorded treaty benefits. For example, RICs, REITs and REMICs are all residents of the United States for purposes of the treaty. Although the income earned by these entities normally is not subject to U.S. tax in the hands of the entity, they are taxable to the extent that they do not currently distribute their profits, and therefore may be regarded as "liable to tax." They also must satisfy a number of requirements under the Code in order to be entitled to special tax treatment.

It is also generally accepted that an entity that would be liable for tax as a resident under the internal law of a state but for a specific exemption from tax (either complete or partial) is a resident of that state for purposes of paragraph 1. The practice of including as residents organizations that are generally exempt from tax reflects the fact that under U.S. law, certain organizations that generally are considered to be tax-exempt entities may be subject to certain excise taxes or to income tax on their unrelated business income. Thus, a U.S. pension trust, or an exempt section 501(c) organization (such as a U.S. charity) that is generally exempt from tax under U.S. law is considered a resident of the United States for all purposes of the treaty.

Paragraph 1 provides that a person who is liable to tax in a Contracting State only in respect of income from sources within that State will not be treated as a resident of that Contracting State for purposes of the Convention. Thus, a consular official of Thailand who is posted in the United States, who may be subject to U.S. tax on U.S. source investment income, but is not taxable in the United States on non-U.S. source income, would not be considered a resident of the United States for purposes of the Convention. (See Code section 7701(b)(5)(B)). Similarly, although not stated explicitly in this Article, an enterprise of Thailand with a permanent establishment in the United States is not, by virtue of that permanent establishment, a resident of the United States. The enterprise generally is subject to U.S. tax only with respect to its income that is attributable to the U.S. permanent establishment, not with respect to its worldwide income, as is a U.S. resident.

A U.S. citizen or a nonresident alien lawfully admitted for permanent residence (a "green card" holder), who is not a resident of Thailand under paragraph 1, will be treated as a U.S. resident for purposes of the Convention only if such individual has a substantial presence, permanent home or habitual abode in the United States. If such an individual is also a resident of Thailand, he shall be considered a resident of both Contracting States and his residence for purposes of this convention shall be determined under paragraph 2. Thus, a U.S. citizen or "green card" holder who has no substantial presence, permanent home, or habitual abode in either Contracting State generally will not be entitled to benefits under the Convention. (However, as noted above in connection with Article 1 (Personal Scope), limited Convention benefits are available to certain persons who are not residents of either Contracting State.)

Special problems are presented by fiscally transparent entities such as partnerships and certain estates and trusts that are not subject to tax at the entity level because they are treated as fiscally transparent under the laws of either Contracting State. Entities falling under this description in the United States would include partnerships, common investment trusts under section 584, grantor trusts and U.S. limited liability companies ("LLC's") that are treated as partnerships for U.S. tax purposes.

It is our understanding that an item of income derived through such fiscally transparent entities will be considered to be derived by a resident of a Contracting State if the resident is treated under the taxation laws of the State where he is resident as deriving the item of income.

For example, if a Thailand corporation distributes a dividend to an entity that is treated as fiscally transparent for U.S. tax purposes, the dividend will be considered to be derived by a resident of the U.S. only to the extent that U.S. tax law treats one or more U.S. residents (whose status as U.S. residents is determined, for this purpose, under U.S. tax law) as deriving the dividend income for U.S. tax purposes. In the case of a partnership, the persons who are, under U.S. tax law, treated as partners of the entity would normally be the persons whom the U.S. tax law would treat as deriving the dividend income through the partnership. Also, it follows that partners whom the U.S. treats as deriving the dividend income for U.S. tax purposes but who are not U.S. residents under U.S. tax law may not claim a benefit for the dividend paid to the entity under the Convention, because they are not residents of the United States for purposes of claiming this treaty benefit. (If, however, the country in which they are treated as resident for tax purposes, as determined under the laws of that country, has an income tax convention with Thailand, they may be entitled to claim a benefit under that convention.) In contrast, if, for example, an entity is organized under U.S. laws and is classified as a corporation for U.S. tax purposes, dividends paid by a Thailand corporation to the U.S. entity will be considered derived by a resident of the United States since the U.S. corporation is treated under U.S. taxation laws as a resident of the United States and as deriving the income.

These results would obtain even if the entity were viewed differently under the tax laws of Thailand (e.g., as not fiscally transparent in the first example above where the entity is treated as a partnership for U.S. tax purposes or as fiscally transparent in the second example where the entity is viewed as not fiscally transparent for U.S. tax purposes). Similarly, the characterization of the entity in a third country is also irrelevant, even if the entity is organized in that third country. The results obtain regardless of whether the entity is disregarded as a separate entity under the laws of one jurisdiction but not the other, such as a single owner entity that is viewed as a branch for U.S. tax purposes and as a corporation for Thai tax purposes. The results also obtain regardless of where the entity is organized, i.e., in the United States, in Thailand, or in a third country.

For example, income from Thailand sources received by an entity organized under the laws of Thailand, which is treated for U.S. tax purposes as a corporation and is owned by a U.S. shareholder who is a U.S. resident for U.S. tax purposes, is not considered derived by the shareholder of that corporation even if, under the tax laws of Thailand, the entity is treated as fiscally transparent. Rather, for purposes of the Convention, the income is treated as derived by the Thai entity.

The rule also applies to trusts to the extent that they are fiscally transparent in either Contracting State. For example, if X, a resident of Thailand, creates a revocable trust and names persons resident in a third country as the beneficiaries of the trust, X would be treated as the beneficial owner of income derived from the United States under the Code's rules. If Thailand has no rules comparable to those in sections 671 through 679 of the Code then it is possible that under Thai law neither X nor the trust would be taxed on the income derived from the United States. In these cases it is to be understood that the trust's income would be regarded as being derived by a resident of Thailand only to the extent that the laws of Thailand treat Thai residents as deriving the income for tax purposes.

The taxation laws of a Contracting State may treat an item of income, profit or gain as income, profit or gain of a resident of that State even if the resident is not subject to tax on that particular item of income, profit or gain. For example, if a Contracting State has a participation exemption for certain foreign-source dividends and capital gains, such income or gains would be regarded as income or gain of a resident of that State who otherwise derived the income or gain, despite the fact that the resident could be exempt from tax in that State on the income or gain.

Income will be considered derived through a fiscally transparent entity if the entity's participation in the transaction giving rise to the income, profit or gain in question is respected after application of any source State anti-abuse principles based on substance over form and similar analyses. For example, if a partnership with U.S. partners receives income arising in the other Contracting State, that income will be considered to be derived through the partnership by its partners as long as the partnership's participation in the transaction is not disregarded for lack of economic substance. In such a case, the partners would be considered to be the beneficial owners of the income.

Paragraph 2

If, under the laws of the two Contracting States, and, thus, under paragraph 1, an individual is deemed to be a resident of both Contracting States, a series of tie-breaker rules are provided in paragraph 2 to determine a single State of residence for that individual. These tests are to be applied in the order in which they are stated. The first test is based on where the individual has a permanent home. If that test is inconclusive because the individual has a permanent home available to him in both States, he will be considered to be a resident of the Contracting State where his personal and economic relations are closest (i.e., the location of his "center of vital interests"). If that test is also inconclusive, or if he does not have a permanent home available to him in either State, he will be treated as a resident of the Contracting State where he maintains an habitual abode. If he has an habitual abode in both States or in neither of them, he will be treated as a resident of his Contracting State of citizenship. If he is a citizen of both States or of neither, the matter will be considered by the competent authorities, who will assign a single State of residence.

Paragraph 3

Paragraph 3 settles dual-residence issues for persons other than individuals. A corporation is resident in the United States if it is created or organized under the laws of the United States or a political subdivision thereof. In Thailand, a corporation is treated as a resident of Thailand if it is incorporated there. Since the same test is used to determine corporate residence under the laws of the United States and under the laws of Thailand, dual corporate residence will not occur. If a person other than an individual or company is resident in both Contracting States, the competent authorities shall determine by mutual agreement a single State of residence for that person for purposes of the convention.

Article 5 (Permanent Establishment)

This Article defines the term "permanent establishment," a term that is significant for several articles of the Convention. The existence of a permanent establishment in a Contracting State is necessary under Article 7 (Business Profits) for the taxation by that State of the business profits of a resident of the other Contracting State. Since the term "fixed base" in Article 15

(Independent Personal Services) is understood by reference to the definition of "permanent establishment," this Article is also relevant for purposes of Article 15. Articles 10, 11 and 12 (dealing with dividends, interest, and royalties, respectively) provide for reduced rates of tax at source on payments of these items of income to a resident of the other State only when the income is not attributable to a permanent establishment or fixed base that the recipient has in the source State. The concept is also relevant in determining when a Contracting State may impose a branch tax under Article 14 (Branch Tax) and certain "other income" under Article 24 (Other Income).

Paragraph 1

The basic definition of the term "permanent establishment" is contained in paragraph 1. As used in the Convention, the term means a fixed place of business through which the business of an enterprise is wholly or partly carried on.

Paragraph 2

Paragraph 2 lists a number of types of fixed places of business that constitute a permanent establishment. This list is illustrative and non-exclusive. According to paragraph 2, the term permanent establishment includes a place of management, a branch, an office, a factory, a workshop, a warehouse, in relation to a person performing storage facilities for others, and a mine, oil or gas well, quarry or other place of extraction of natural resources. As indicated in the OECD Commentaries (see paragraphs 4 through 8), a general principle to be observed in determining whether a permanent establishment exists under paragraphs 1 and 2 is that the place of business must be "fixed" in the sense that a particular building or physical location is used by the enterprise for the conduct of its business, and that it must be foreseeable that the enterprise's use of this building or other physical location will be more than temporary. The use of singular nouns in this illustrative list is not meant to imply that each such place of business constitutes a separate permanent establishment. In the case of mines or wells, for example, several such places of business could constitute a single permanent establishment if the project forms a commercial and geographical whole.

Paragraph 3

Paragraph 3 describes several additional activities or business sites that will constitute a permanent establishment. Paragraph 3(a) adds that the term "permanent establishment" may include a building site or a construction, assembly or installation project, or supervisory activities connected with such sites or projects. It may include, as well, a drilling rig or ship used for the exploration or exploitation of natural resources. The sites or activities described in subparagraph (a) will constitute a permanent establishment only if they continue for a period or periods aggregating more than 120 days within any twelve-month period. This limit does not apply to the site of the actual production of oil or gas from a well or any other place of extraction of natural resources, because such activity is dealt with in subparagraph (g) of paragraph 2.

The 120-day test applies separately to each site or project. The count of days for purposes of the 120-day threshold begins when work (including preparatory work carried on by the enterprise) physically begins in a Contracting State. A series of contracts or projects by a contractor that are interdependent both commercially and geographically are to be treated as a single project for purposes of applying the 120-day threshold test. For example, the construction of a housing development would be considered as a single project even if each house were constructed for a different purchaser. Several drilling rigs operated by a drilling contractor in the same sector of the continental shelf also normally would be treated as a single project.

If the 120-day threshold is exceeded in a twelve-month period, the site or project constitutes a permanent establishment from the first day of activity within that twelve-month period. In applying this paragraph, time spent by a sub-contractor on a building site is counted as time spent by the general contractor at the site for purposes of determining whether the general contractor has a permanent establishment. However, for the sub-contractor itself to be treated as having a permanent establishment, the sub-contractor's activities at the site must last for more than 120 days within any twelve-month period. If a sub-contractor is on a site intermittently time is measured from the first day the sub-contractor is on the site until the last day (i.e., intervening days that the sub-contractor is not on the site are counted) for purposes of applying the 120-day rule.

These interpretations of paragraph 3(a) are based on the Commentary to paragraph 3 of Article 5 of the OECD Model, which contains language similar to that in the Convention (except for the absence in the OECD Model of a rule for drilling rigs). These interpretations are consistent with the generally accepted international interpretation of the language in paragraph 3(a) of Article 5 of the Convention.

Paragraph 3(b) provides that the term "permanent establishment" encompasses the furnishing of services, including consultancy services, by an enterprise of a Contracting State through its employees or any other personnel engaged for that purpose if one of two tests are satisfied. The activities will constitute a permanent establishment only if (1) the activities for the same or a connected project continue within a State for a period or periods aggregating more than 90 days within any twelve-month period, or, (2) the services are performed within a State for a related enterprise within the meaning of paragraph 1 of Article 9, in which case no time threshold must be met. Services rendered for an unrelated enterprise within the country for a period or periods aggregating less than 30 days in any taxable year will not cause a permanent establishment to exist in that taxable year. That time will count, however, in determining whether the 90-day test has been met. Thus, if services are performed in Thailand on behalf of a U.S. enterprise for 20 days at the end of year 1, continuing for an additional 80 days at the beginning of year 2, a permanent establishment would exist in Thailand, because the 90-day threshold has been passed, but there would be a permanent establishment only in year 2, and not in year 1, and, thus, only the income of year two would be subject to tax in Thailand. As with respect to the 120-day threshold discussed above, the count of days for purposes of the 90-day threshold begins when work (including preparatory work carried on by the enterprise) begins in a Contracting State.

Paragraph 4

This paragraph contains exceptions to the general rule of paragraph 1, listing a number of activities that may be carried on through a fixed place of business, but which nevertheless do not create a permanent establishment. The use of facilities solely to store or display merchandise belonging to an enterprise does not constitute a permanent establishment of that enterprise. The maintenance of a stock of goods belonging to an enterprise solely for the purpose of storage or display, or solely for the purpose of processing by another enterprise does not give rise to a permanent establishment of the first-mentioned enterprise. The maintenance of a fixed place of business solely for the purpose of purchasing goods or merchandise, or for collecting information, for the enterprise, or for other activities that have a preparatory or auxiliary character for the enterprise, such as advertising, or the supply of information do not constitute a permanent establishment of the enterprise. Thus, for example, an employee of a U.S. manufacturer gathering information as part of a market research project would not constitute a permanent establishment of the manufacturer, even if the activity takes place through a fixed place of business. Similarly, as explained in paragraph 22 of the OECD Commentaries, an employee of a news organization engaged merely in gathering information would not constitute a permanent establishment of the news organization.

Paragraph 5

Unlike the U.S. and OECD Models, subparagraphs (a) and (b) of paragraph 4 do not carve out the use of facilities or the maintenance of a stock of goods solely for the purpose of delivery from constituting a permanent establishment. Paragraph (5), however, adds that the term "permanent establishment" shall be deemed not to include the use of facilities or the maintenance of a stock of goods or merchandise for the purpose of occasional delivery of such goods or merchandise. A permanent establishment does exist if deliveries are made on a regular basis from a warehouse or other storage facility.

Paragraph 6

Paragraphs 6 and 7 specify when activities carried on by an agent on behalf of an enterprise create a permanent establishment of that enterprise. Paragraph 6 sets forth three conditions under which a dependent agent of an enterprise is deemed to constitute a permanent establishment of the enterprise. The enterprise will have a permanent establishment in a State if the agent has and regularly exercises in that State an authority to conclude contracts that are binding on the enterprise. If, however, his activities are limited to those activities specified in paragraphs 4 and 5 which would not constitute a permanent establishment if carried on by the enterprise through a fixed place of business, the agent is not a permanent establishment of the enterprise. The enterprise also will have a permanent establishment in that State if the agent regularly secures orders in that State for the enterprise, even if the agent has no authority to conclude contracts on behalf of the enterprise. In addition, the enterprise will have a permanent establishment in that State if the agent maintains a stock of goods or merchandise belonging to that enterprise in that State for the enterprise from which the agent regularly makes deliveries on behalf of the enterprise.

Paragraph 7

Under paragraph 7, an enterprise is not deemed to have a permanent establishment in a Contracting State merely because it carries on business in that State through an independent agent, including a broker or general commission agent, if the agent is acting in the ordinary course of his business as an independent agent. Thus, there are two conditions that must be satisfied: the agent must be both legally and economically independent of the enterprise, and the agent must be acting in the ordinary course of its business in carrying out activities on behalf of the enterprise.

Whether the agent and the enterprise are independent is a factual determination. Among the questions to be considered are the extent to which the agent operates on the basis of instructions from the enterprise. An agent that is subject to detailed instructions regarding the conduct of its operations or comprehensive control by the enterprise is not legally independent.

In determining whether the agent is economically independent, a relevant factor is the extent to which the agent bears business risk. Business risk refers primarily to risk of loss. An independent agent typically bears risk of loss from its own activities. In the absence of other factors that would establish dependence, an agent that shares business risk with the enterprise, or has its own business risk, is economically independent because its business activities are not integrated with those of the principal. Conversely, an agent that bears little or no risk from that activities it performs is not economically independent and therefore is not described in paragraph 7.

Another relevant factor in determining whether an agent is economically independent is whether the agent has an exclusive or nearly exclusive relationship with the principal. Such a relationship may indicate that the principal has economic control over the agent. A number of principals acting in concert also may have economic control over the agent. The limited scope of the agent's activities and the agent's dependence on a single source of income may indicate that the agent lacks economic independence. Unlike the comparable provisions in the U.S. Model, paragraph 7 provides that an agent will not be considered to be an independent agent within the meaning of paragraph 7 when, by agreement between the agent and the enterprise, the activities of the agent are devoted wholly or almost wholly on behalf of that enterprise or other enterprises controlling, or controlled by, that enterprise. It should be borne in mind, however, that, in the absence of such an agreement between the agent and the enterprise, exclusivity is not in itself a conclusive test: an agent may be economically independent notwithstanding an exclusive relationship with the principal if it has the capacity to diversify and acquire other clients without substantial modifications to its current business and without substantial harm to its business profits. Thus, exclusivity should be viewed as a pointer to further investigation of the relationship between the principal and the agent. Each case must be addressed on the basis of its own facts and circumstances.

Paragraph 8

Paragraph 8 clarifies that a company that is a resident of a Contracting State is not deemed to have a permanent establishment in the other Contracting State merely because it controls, or is controlled by, a company that is a resident of that other Contracting State, or that carries on business in that other Contracting State. The determination whether a permanent establishment exists is made solely on the basis of the factors described in paragraphs 1 through 7 of the Article. Whether a company is a permanent establishment of a related company, therefore, is based solely on those factors and not on the ownership or control relationship between the companies.

Article 6 (Income from Immovable (Real) Property)

This Article deals with the taxation of income from immovable, or real, property. The two terms should be understood to have the same meaning.

Paragraph 1

The first paragraph of Article 6 states the general rule that income of a resident of a Contracting State derived from real property situated in the other Contracting State may be taxed in the Contracting State in which the property is situated. The paragraph specifies that income from real property includes income from agriculture and forestry. Paragraph 3 clarifies that the income referred to in paragraph 1 also means income from any use of real property, including, but not limited to, income from direct use by the owner (in which case income may be imputed to the owner for tax purposes) and rental income from the letting of real property.

This Article does not grant an exclusive taxing right to the situs State; the situs State is merely given the primary right to tax. The Article does not impose any limitation in terms of rate or form of tax on the situs State.

Paragraph 2

The terms "immovable property" or "real property" are defined in paragraph 2 by reference to the internal law definition in the situs State. In the case of the United States, the term has the meaning given to it by Treas. Reg. § 1.897-1(b). In addition, paragraph 2 specifies certain classes of property, including rights, that, regardless of domestic law definitions, are to be included within the meaning of the terms for purposes of the Convention. It also specifies that the terms do not include ships, boats, or aircraft in any event.

Paragraph 3

Paragraph 3 makes clear that all forms of income derived from the exploitation of real property are taxable in the Contracting State in which the property is situated. In the case of a net lease of real property, if a net election has not been made, the gross rental payment (before deductible expenses incurred by the lessee) is treated as income from the property. Income from the disposition of an interest in real property, however, is not considered "derived" from real property and is not dealt with in this article. The taxation of that income is addressed in Article 13 (Gains). Also, the interest paid on a mortgage on real property and distributions by a U.S. Real Estate Investment Trust are not dealt with in Article 6. Such payments would fall under Articles 10 (Dividends), 11 (Interest) or 13 (Gains). Finally, dividends paid by a United States Real Property Holding Corporation are not considered to be income from the exploitation of real property: such payments would fall under Article 10 (Dividends) or 13(Gains).

Paragraph 4

This paragraph specifies that the basic rule of paragraph 1 (as elaborated in paragraph 3) applies to income from real property of an enterprise and to income from real property used for the performance of independent personal services. This clarifies that the situs country may tax the real property income (including rental income) of a resident of the other Contracting State in the absence of attribution to a permanent establishment or fixed base in the situs State. This provision represents an exception to the general rule under Articles 7 (Business Profits) and 15 (Independent Personal Services) that income must be attributable to a permanent establishment or fixed base, respectively, in order to be taxable in the situs state.

Article 7 (Business Profits)

This Article provides rules for the taxation by a Contracting State of the business profits of an enterprise of the other Contracting State.

Paragraph 1

Paragraph 1 states the general rule that business profits (as defined in paragraph 8) of an enterprise of one Contracting State may not be taxed by the other Contracting State unless the enterprise carries on business in that other Contracting State through a permanent establishment (as defined in Article 5 (Permanent Establishment)) situated there. If the enterprise has a permanent establishment in the other Contracting State, that other State may tax the portion of the enterprise's business profits which is attributable to the permanent establishment itself (subparagraph 1(a)). Under certain circumstances, the State in which the permanent establishment exists may also tax income of the enterprise attributable to sales in that other State of goods or merchandise of the same kind as those sold through the permanent establishment (subparagraph 1(b)), or to other business transactions carried on in that other State which are of the same or similar kind as those effected through the permanent establishment (subparagraph 1(c)). The rules in subparagraphs (b) and (c) are of a type known as "limited force of attraction" rules.

This limited force of attraction rule is similar to, but narrower than, a rule found in the U.N. Model. Under the rule in the U.N. Model, if an enterprise of one Contracting State derives income from the sale of goods or the carrying on of other business activities through a permanent establishment situated in the other Contracting State, income derived directly by the enterprise (i.e., not through the permanent establishment) from the sale of goods of the same or similar kind as those sold through the permanent establishment or from the carrying on of activities of the same or similar kind as those carried on through the permanent establishment may be attributed to the permanent establishment. Countries that insist on including a limited force of attraction rule see it as a means of preventing avoidance of their tax at source. The force of attraction rule in this Convention focuses on its anti-abuse function. Its application is limited to situations in which it can be shown that the transaction giving rise to the income was carried out outside the permanent establishment in order to avoid taxation in the country in which the permanent establishment is situated. For example, if the Bangkok office of a U.S. consulting firm provides certain services to small companies in Thailand and a very large Thai company requires similar services but on a scale too large for the permanent establishment to handle, the Thai company might enter into a contract with the consulting firm's home office in the United States to provide those services directly. The income from that transaction would not be attributed to the permanent establishment because it could not be shown that the transaction was structured through the U.S. office in order to avoid Thai tax. If, however, some small Thai companies are served by the Bangkok office and other similar-sized companies are served directly from the United States, it might be possible to show that services were carried out through the home office to avoid Thai tax. If such a case were made, the income from these contracts with the home office would be attributed to the permanent establishment.

The limited force of attraction rule in this Convention is narrower than the rule of Code section 864(c)(3).

Paragraph 2

Paragraph 2 provides rules for the attribution of business profits to a permanent establishment. The Contracting States will attribute to a permanent establishment the profits that it would have earned had it been an independent enterprise engaged in the same or similar activities under the same or similar circumstances. This language incorporates the arm's-length standard for purposes of determining the profits attributable to a permanent establishment. The computation of business profits attributable to a permanent establishment under this paragraph is subject to the rules of paragraph 3 for the allowance of expenses incurred for the purposes of earning the profits.

The "attributable to" concept of paragraph 2 is analogous but not entirely equivalent to the "effectively connected" concept in Code section 864(c). The profits attributable to a permanent establishment may be from sources within or without a Contracting State. Thus, for example, items of income described in section 864(c)(4) of the Code which are "attributable to" a permanent establishment in the United States are subject to tax by the United States. In addition, the "attributable to" concept does not incorporate the limited force of attraction rule of Code section 864(c)(3), although the concept is subject to the limited force of attraction rules of subparagraphs 1(b) and 1(c) described above.

Paragraph 3

Paragraph 3 provides that in determining the business profits of a permanent establishment, deductions shall be allowed for the expenses incurred for the purposes of the permanent establishment, ensuring that business profits will be taxed on a net basis. This rule is not limited to expenses incurred exclusively for the purposes of the permanent establishment, but includes a reasonable allocation or apportionment of executive and general administrative expenses incurred for the purposes of the enterprise as a whole, or that part of the enterprise that includes the permanent establishment. Deductions are to be allowed regardless of which accounting unit of the enterprise books the expenses, so long as they are incurred for the purposes of the permanent establishment. For example, a portion of the general administrative expense recorded on the books of the home office in one State may be deducted by a permanent establishment in the other if properly allocable thereto.

The paragraph specifies that the expenses that may be considered to be incurred for the purposes of the permanent establishment include a reasonable amount of executive and general administrative expenses. Unlike the U.S. Model, the paragraph does not specify that research and development expenses and interest may also be allocated on a reasonable basis, but this is understood to be implicit. This rule permits (but does not require) each Contracting State to apply the type of expense allocation rules provided by U.S. law (such as in Treas. Reg. sections 1.861-8 and 1.882-5).

Paragraph 3 does not permit a deduction for expenses charged to a permanent establishment by another unit of the enterprise. Thus, a permanent establishment may not deduct a royalty deemed paid to the head office. Similarly, a permanent establishment may not increase its business profits by the amount of any notional fees for ancillary services performed for another unit of the enterprise, but also should not receive a deduction for the expense of providing such services, since those expenses would be incurred for purposes of a business unit other than the permanent establishment.

Paragraph 4

Paragraph 4 of this Article corresponds to paragraph 4 of Article 7 of the OECD Model. The paragraph provides that a Contracting State may, where it is customary to do so under its law and practice, determine the profits attributable to a permanent establishment on the basis of an apportionment of the total profits of the enterprise. The paragraph clearly states, however, that any such approach must be designed to approximate an arm's-length result.

Paragraph 5

Paragraph 5 provides that no business profits can be attributed to a permanent establishment merely because it purchases goods or merchandise for the enterprise of which it is a part. This rule applies only to an office that performs functions for the enterprise in addition to purchasing. The income attribution issue does not arise if the sole activity of the office in the host State is the purchase of goods or merchandise because such activity does not give rise to a permanent establishment under Article 5 (Permanent Establishment). A common situation in which paragraph 5 is relevant is one in which a permanent establishment purchases raw materials for the enterprise's manufacturing operation conducted outside the United States and sells the manufactured product. While business profits may be attributable to the permanent establishment with respect to its sales activities, no profits are attributable to it with respect to its purchasing activities.

Paragraph 6

Paragraph 6 provides that profits shall be determined by the same method of accounting each year, unless there is good reason to change the method used. This rule assures consistent tax treatment over time for permanent establishments. It limits the ability of both the Contracting State and the enterprise to change accounting methods to be applied to the permanent establishment. It does not, however, restrict a Contracting State from imposing additional requirements, such as the rules under Code section 481, to prevent amounts from being duplicated or omitted following a change in accounting method.

Paragraph 7

Paragraph 7 coordinates the provisions of Article 7 and other provisions of the Convention. Under this paragraph, when business profits include items of income that are dealt with separately under other articles of the Convention, the provisions of those articles will, except when they specifically provide to the contrary, take precedence over the provisions of Article 7. For example, the taxation of dividends will be determined by the rules of Article 10 (Dividends), and not by Article 7, except where, as provided in paragraph 5 of Article 10, the dividend is attributable to a permanent establishment or fixed base. In the latter case the provisions of Articles 7 or 15 (Independent Personal Services) apply. Thus, an enterprise of one State deriving dividends from the other State may not rely on Article 7 to exempt those dividends from tax at source if they are not attributable to a permanent establishment of the enterprise in the other State. By the same token, if the dividends are attributable to a permanent establishment in the other State, the dividends may be taxed on a net income basis at the source State's full corporate tax rate, rather than on a gross basis under Article 10 (Dividends).

As provided in Article 8 (Shipping and Air Transport), income derived from shipping and air transport activities in international traffic and rental income incidental to such international transport described in that Article is taxable, or exempt, only under the provisions of Article 8, irrespective of whether it is attributable to a permanent establishment situated in the source State.

Paragraph 8

The term "business profits" is defined generally in paragraph 8 to mean income derived from any trade or business.

In accordance with this broad definition, the term "business profits" is understood to include income attributable to notional principal contracts and other financial instruments to the extent that the income is attributable to a trade or business of dealing in such instruments, or is otherwise related to a trade or business (as in the case of a notional principal contract entered into for the purpose of hedging currency risk arising from an active trade or business). Any other income derived from such instruments is, unless specifically covered in another article, dealt with under Article 24 (Other Income).

Income earned by an enterprise from the furnishing of personal services is business profits. Thus, a consulting firm resident in one State whose employees perform services in the other State through a permanent establishment may be taxed in that other State on a net basis under Article 7, and not under Article 15 (Independent Personal Services), which applies only to individuals. The salaries of the employees would be subject to the rules of Article 16 (Dependent Personal Services).

The paragraph specifies that the term "business profits" includes income derived by an enterprise from the rental of ships, aircraft, and containers, including trailers, barges and related equipment for the transport of containers if such income is not incidental to income from the operation of ships or aircraft in international traffic (in which case it would be subject to Article 8 (Shipping and Air Transport)). The inclusion of such in business profits means that such income earned by a resident of a Contacting State can taxed by the other Contracting State only if the income is attributable to a permanent establishment in that other State, and, if the income is taxable, it can taxed only on a net basis.

Paragraph 9

Paragraph 9 incorporates into the Convention the rule of Code section 864(c)(6). Like the Code section on which it is based, paragraph 8 provides that any income or gain attributable to a permanent establishment or a fixed base during its existence is taxable in the Contracting State where the permanent establishment or fixed base is situated, even if the payment of that income or gain is deferred until after the permanent establishment or fixed base ceases to exist. This rule applies with respect to paragraphs 1 and 2 of Article 7 (Business Profits), paragraph 5 of Article 10 (Dividends), paragraph 5 of Article 11 (Interest), paragraph 4 of Article 12 (Royalties), and paragraph 1(a) of Article 15 (Independent Personal Services) and paragraph 2 of Article 24 (Other Income).

Relation to Other Articles

This Article is subject to the saving clause of paragraph 2 of Article 1 (Personal Scope). Thus, if a citizen of the United States who is a resident of Thailand under the treaty derives business profits from the United States that are not attributable to a permanent establishment in the United States, the United States may tax those profits, notwithstanding the provision of paragraph 1 of this Article which would exempt the income from U.S. tax.

The benefits of this Article are also subject to Article 18 (Limitation on Benefits). Thus, an enterprise of Thailand that derives income effectively connected with a U.S. trade or business that does not constitute a permanent establishment under Article 5, may not claim the benefits of Article 7 unless the resident carrying on the enterprise qualifies for such benefits under Article 18.

Article 8 (Shipping and Air Transport)

This Article governs the taxation of profits from the operation of ships and aircraft in international traffic. The term "international traffic" is defined in subparagraph 1(d) of Article 3 (General Definitions).

Paragraph 1

Subparagraphs 1(a) and (b) provide, for United States and Thai residents, respectively, that profits derived by a resident of a Contracting State from the operation of aircraft in international traffic are taxable only in that Contracting State. Because paragraph 7 of Article 7 (Business Profits) defers to Article 8 with respect to shipping income, such income derived by a resident of one of the Contracting States may not be taxed in the other State even if the resident has a permanent establishment in that other State. Thus, if a U.S. airline has a ticket office in Thailand, Thailand may not tax the airline's profits attributable to that office under Article 7. Unlike most treaties, however, the exclusive residence State taxation rule applies only to income from the operation of aircraft in international traffic, and not to income from the operation of ships.

Paragraph 2

Paragraph 2 provides for limited source country taxation of income from the operation of ships in international traffic. Under this paragraph, the amount of tax that may be imposed by a Contracting State on profits derived by an enterprise of the other Contracting State from the operation of ships in international traffic shall be reduced to 50 percent of the amount which would have been imposed in the absence of the Convention. Thus, for example, under subparagraph 2(b) the U.S. tax on the income of a Thai shipping company from the operation of ships in international traffic would be limited to a maximum of 2 percent of the company's U.S.

source gross transportation income from such operation (under section 887 of the Code, the tax rate is 4 percent).

Paragraph 3

Paragraph 3 provides that income from the operation of ships or aircraft in international traffic also includes income from the rental of ships or aircraft if such rental income is incidental to income described in paragraphs 1 or 2. Income from the rental of ships or aircraft is incidental to income from the operation of ships or aircraft in international traffic if the lessor is a shipping company or airline, and the ship or aircraft is part of the body of equipment used by the lessor in its business as an international carrier. Such rental income, therefore, is treated the same as income from the operation of aircraft and ships under paragraphs 1 and 2, respectively. Income from the incidental rental of aircraft is taxable only by the State of residence of the lessor. Income from the incidental rental of ships is taxable also by the source country only to the extent of one-half of the tax that would be imposed in the absence of the Convention.

In addition, income of a resident of a Contracting State from the rental of ships or aircraft on a full basis (i.e., with crew) when such ships or aircraft are used in international traffic is treated as income of the lessor from the operation of ships and aircraft in international traffic and, therefore, is exempt, in the case of aircraft, or taxable to the extent of one-half the otherwise applicable tax in the case of ships, under paragraphs 1 and 2 respectively.

Paragraph 3 does not specify, as does the comparable paragraph in the U.S. Model (paragraph 2), that income earned by an enterprise from the inland transport of property or passengers within either Contracting State falls within Article 8 if the transport is undertaken as part of the international transport of property or passengers by the enterprise. The Convention language is to be interpreted to mean the same as language in the U.S. Model, as evidenced by the discussion in this Technical Explanation of the definition of international traffic in paragraph 1 of Article 3, even though the language of the U.S. Model definition and the Convention definition differ. Thus, if a U.S. shipping company contracts to carry property from Thailand to a U.S. city and, as part of that contract, it transports the property by truck from its point of origin in Thailand to a Thai airport (or it contracts with a trucking company to carry the property to the airport) the income earned by the U.S. shipping company from the overland leg of the journey would be taxable only in the United States under paragraph 1 if the international transport is by air. It would be subject in Thailand to half of the Thai tax otherwise applicable, under the provisions of paragraph 2, if the international transport is by ship. Similarly, Article 8 also would apply to income from lighterage undertaken as part of the international transport of goods.

Finally, certain non-transport activities that are an integral part of the services performed by a transport company are understood to be covered in paragraphs 1 and 2, though they are not specified in paragraph 3. These include, for example, the performance of some maintenance or catering services by one airline for another airline, if these services are incidental to the provision of those services by the airline for itself. Income earned by concessionaires, however, is not covered by Article 8. These interpretations of paragraphs 1 and 2 also are consistent with the Commentary to Article 8 of the OECD Model.

Paragraph 4

Paragraph 4 provides that income from the use, maintenance, or rental of containers (including equipment for their transport) that is incidental to income from the operation of ships or aircraft in international traffic is treated as income from the operation of ships or aircraft in international traffic described in paragraphs 1 or 2. Thus, income from the use, maintenance or rental of containers by a shipping or airline company, where those containers are part of the equipment used by that company in international traffic, is subject to tax under the rules of paragraphs 1 and 2, as appropriate. For example, income from the rental of containers by an airline is taxable only in the country of residence of the airline. Income from the rental of containers by a shipping company therefore is taxable by the source country; under this Article, however, it is taxable at a rate no more than 50 percent of the tax that would be imposed in the absence of the Convention.

Income from the use, maintenance or rental of containers that is not incidental to the operation of ships or aircraft in international traffic is treated as business profits under the definition in paragraph 8 of Article 7 (Business Profits). It is taxable by the source State, therefore, on a net basis, and only when attributable to a permanent establishment in that State.

Paragraph 5

Paragraph 5 clarifies that the provisions of paragraphs 1, 2 and 4 also apply to profits derived by an enterprise of a Contracting State from participation in a pool, joint business or international operating agency. This refers to various arrangements for international cooperation by carriers in shipping and air transport. For example, airlines from the United States and Thailand may agree to share the transport of passengers between the two countries. They each will fly the same number of flights per week and share the revenues from that route equally, regardless of the number of passengers that each airline actually transports. Paragraph 5 makes clear that with respect to each carrier the income dealt with in the Article is that carrier's share of the total transport, not the income derived from the passengers actually carried by the airline.

Relation to Other Articles

The taxation of gains from the alienation of ships, aircraft or containers is not dealt with in this Article but in paragraph 2 of Article 13 (Gains).

As with other benefits of the Convention, the benefit of exclusive residence country taxation or limited source-country taxation under Article 8 is available to an enterprise only if it is entitled to benefits under Article 18 (Limitation on Benefits).

This Article also is subject to the saving clause of paragraph 2 of Article 1 (Personal Scope). Thus, if a citizen of the United States who is a resident of Thailand derives profits from the operation of aircraft in international traffic, notwithstanding the exclusive residence country taxation in paragraph 1 of Article 8, the United States may tax those profits as part of the worldwide income of the citizen.

Exchange of Notes

Diplomatic Notes exchanged at the time of the signing of the Convention, stated the understanding that if Thailand agrees in a treaty or other agreement with any other country to (1) a rate of tax on income or profits derived by residents of such other country on the operation of ships that is lower than the rate specified in paragraph 2 (i.e., less than 50 percent of the tax otherwise applicable), or (2) treatment for the rental or use of containers in international traffic that is more favorable than the treatment specified in paragraph 8 of Article 7 (Business Profits) or paragraph 4 of Article 8 (Shipping and Air Transport), then Thailand will agree to reopen negotiations with the United States with a view to the conclusion of a Protocol which would extend such lower rate or more favorable treatment to residents of the United States. The agreement stated in these notes to reopen negotiations does not guarantee that agreement on a Protocol will be reached. Any agreement that is reached to amend the Convention will be subject to the normal ratification procedures in both countries.

Article 9 (Associated Enterprises)

This Article incorporates in the Convention the arm's-length principle reflected in the U.S. domestic transfer pricing provisions, particularly Code section 482. It provides that when related enterprises engage in a transaction on terms that are not arm's-length, the Contracting States may make appropriate adjustments to the taxable income and tax liability of such related enterprises to reflect what the income and tax of these enterprises with respect to the transaction would have been had there been an arm's-length relationship between them.

Paragraph 1

This paragraph addresses the situation where an enterprise of a Contracting State is related to an enterprise of the other Contracting State, and there are arrangements or conditions imposed between the enterprises in their commercial or financial relations that are different from those that would have existed in the absence of the relationship. Under these circumstances, the Contracting States may adjust the income (or loss) of the enterprise to reflect what it would have been in the absence of such a relationship.

The paragraph identifies the relationships between enterprises that serve as a prerequisite to application of the Article. The necessary element in these relationships is effective control, which is also the standard for purposes of section 482. Thus, the Article applies if an enterprise of one State participates directly or indirectly in the management, control, or capital of the enterprise of the other State. Also, the Article applies if any third person or persons participate directly or indirectly in the management, control, or capital of enterprises of different States. For this purpose, all types of control are included, i.e., whether or not legally enforceable and however exercised or exercisable.

The fact that a transaction is entered into between such related enterprises does not, in and of itself, mean that a Contracting State may adjust the income (or loss) of one or both of the enterprises under the provisions of this Article. If the conditions of the transaction are consistent with those that would be made between independent persons, the income arising from that transaction should not be subject to adjustment under this Article.

Similarly, the fact that associated enterprises may have concluded arrangements, such as cost sharing arrangements or general services agreements, is not in itself an indication that the two enterprises have entered into a non-arm's-length transaction that should give rise to an adjustment under paragraph 1. Both related and unrelated parties enter into such arrangements (e.g., joint venturers may share some development costs). As with any other kind of transaction, when related parties enter into an arrangement, the specific arrangement must be examined to see whether or not it meets the arm's-length standard. In the event that it does not, an appropriate adjustment may be made, which may include modifying the terms of the agreement or re-characterizing the transaction to reflect its substance.

It is understood that the "commensurate with income" standard for determining appropriate transfer prices for intangibles, added to Code section 482 by the Tax Reform Act of 1986, was designed to operate consistently with the arm's-length standard. The implementation of this standard in the section 482 regulations is in accordance with the general principles of paragraph 1 of Article 9 of the Convention, as interpreted by the OECD Transfer Pricing Guidelines.

It is understood that the adjustments to income provided for in paragraph 1 do not replace, but complement, the adjustments provided for under the internal laws of the Contracting States. Even though it is not stated explicitly in the Convention, the Contracting States preserve their rights to apply internal law provisions relating to adjustments between related parties. They also reserve the right to make adjustments in cases involving tax evasion or fraud. Such adjustments -- the distribution, apportionment, or allocation of income, deductions, credits or allowances -- are permitted even if they are different from, or go beyond, those authorized by paragraph 1 of the Article, as long as they accord with the general principles of paragraph 1, i.e., that the adjustment reflects what would have transpired had the related parties been acting at arm's length. For example, while paragraph 1 explicitly allows adjustments of deductions in computing taxable income, it does not deal with adjustments to tax credits. It does not, however, preclude such adjustments if they can be made under internal law. The OECD Model reaches the same result, as explained in paragraph 4 of the Commentaries to Article 9.

This Article also permits tax authorities to deal with thin capitalization issues. They may, in the context of Article 9, scrutinize more than the rate of interest charged on a loan between related persons. They also may examine the capital structure of an enterprise, whether a payment in respect of that loan should be treated as interest, and, if it is treated as interest, under what circumstances interest deductions should be allowed to the payor. Paragraph 2 of the Commentaries to Article 9 of the OECD Model, together with the U.S. observation set forth in paragraph 15, sets forth a similar understanding of the scope of Article 9 in the context of thin capitalization.

Paragraph 2

When a Contracting State has made an adjustment that is consistent with the provisions of paragraph 1, and the other Contracting State agrees that the adjustment was appropriate to reflect arm's-length conditions, that other Contracting State is obligated to make a correlative adjustment (sometimes referred to as a "corresponding adjustment") to the tax liability of the related person in that other Contracting State.

As explained in the OECD Commentaries, Article 9 leaves the treatment of "secondary adjustments" to the laws of the Contracting States. When an adjustment under Article 9 has been made, one of the parties will have in its possession funds that it would not have had at arm's length. The question arises as to how to treat these funds. In the United States the general practice is to treat such funds as a dividend or contribution to capital, depending on the relationship between the parties. Under certain circumstances, the parties may be permitted to restore the funds to the party that would have the funds at arm's length, and to establish an account payable pending restoration of the funds. See, Rev. Proc. 65-17, 1965-1 C.B. 833.

The Contracting State making a secondary adjustment will take the other provisions of the Convention, where relevant, into account. For example, if the effect of a secondary adjustment is to treat a U.S. corporation as having made a distribution of profits to its parent corporation in Thailand, the provisions of Article 10 (Dividends) will apply, and the United States may impose a 10 percent withholding tax on the dividend. Also, if under Article 25 the other State generally gives a credit for taxes paid with respect to such dividends, it would also be required to do so in this case.

The competent authorities are authorized by paragraph 2 to consult, if necessary, to resolve any differences in the application of these provisions. For example, there may be a disagreement over whether an adjustment made by a Contracting State under paragraph 1 was appropriate.

If a correlative adjustment is made under paragraph 2, it is to be implemented, pursuant to Article 27 (Mutual Agreement Procedure), notwithstanding any time limits or other procedural limitations in the law of the Contracting State making the adjustment. If a taxpayer has entered a closing agreement (or other written settlement) with the United States prior to bringing a case to the competent authorities, the U.S. competent authority will endeavor only to obtain a correlative adjustment from Thailand. See, Rev. Proc. 96-13, 1996-1 C.B. 616, Section 7.05.

Relation to Other Articles

The saving clause of paragraph 2 of Article 1 (Personal Scope) does not apply to paragraph 2 of Article 9 by virtue of the exceptions to the saving clause in paragraph 3(a) of Article 1. Thus, even if the statute of limitations has run, a refund of tax can be made in order to implement a correlative adjustment. Statutory or procedural limitations, however, cannot be overridden to impose additional tax, because paragraph 4 of Article 1 provides that the Convention cannot restrict any statutory benefit.

Article 10 (Dividends)

Article 10 provides rules for the taxation of dividends paid by a company that is a resident of one Contracting State to a beneficial owner that is a resident of the other Contracting State. The article provides for full residence country taxation of such dividends and a limited source-State right to tax.

Paragraph 1

The right of a shareholder's country of residence to tax dividends arising in the source country is preserved by paragraph 1, which permits a Contracting State to tax its residents on dividends paid to them by a company resident in the other Contracting State. For dividends from any other source paid to a resident of a Contracting State, Article 24 (Other Income) grants the residence country exclusive taxing jurisdiction (other than for dividends attributable to a permanent establishment or fixed base in the other State).

Paragraph 2

The State of source may also tax dividends beneficially owned by a resident of the other State, subject to the limitations in paragraphs 2 and 3. Generally, the source State's tax is limited to 15 percent of the gross amount of the dividend paid. If, however, the beneficial owner of the dividends is a company resident in the other State that holds at least 10 percent of the voting power of the company paying the dividend, then the source State's tax is limited to 10 percent of the gross amount of the dividend. Indirect ownership of voting shares (through tiers of corporations) and direct ownership of non-voting shares are not taken into account for purposes of determining eligibility for the 10 percent direct dividend rate. Shares are considered voting shares if they provide the power to elect, appoint or replace any person vested with the powers ordinarily exercised by the board of directors of a U.S. corporation.

The benefits of paragraph 2 may be granted at the time of payment by means of reduced withholding at source. It also is consistent with the paragraph for tax to be withheld at the time of payment at full statutory rates, and the treaty benefit to be granted by means of a subsequent refund.

Paragraph 2 does not affect the taxation of the paying company on the profits out of which the dividends are paid. The taxation by a Contracting State of the income of its resident companies is governed by the internal law of the Contracting State, subject to the provisions of paragraph 4 of Article 26 (Non-Discrimination).

The term "beneficial owner" is not defined in the Convention, and is, therefore, defined as under the internal law of the country imposing tax (i.e., the source country). The beneficial owner of the dividend for purposes of Article 10 is the person to which the dividend income is attributable for tax purposes under the laws of the source State. Thus, if a dividend paid by a corporation that is a resident of one of the States (as determined under Article 4 (Residence)) is received by a nominee or agent that is a resident of the other State on behalf of a person that is not a resident of that other State, the dividend is not entitled to the benefits of this Article. However, a dividend received by a nominee on behalf of a resident of that other State would be entitled to benefits. Further, in accordance with paragraph 12 of the OECD Commentaries to Article 10, the source State may disregard as beneficial owner certain persons that nominally may receive a dividend but in substance do not control it. See also, paragraph 24 of the OECD Commentaries to Article 1 (General Scope).

Companies holding shares through fiscally transparent entities such as partnerships are considered for purposes of this paragraph to hold their proportionate interest in the shares held by the intermediate entity. As a result, companies holding shares through such entities may be able to claim the benefits of subparagraph (a) under certain circumstances. The lower rate applies when the company's proportionate share of the shares held by the intermediate entity meets the 10 percent voting stock threshold. Whether this ownership threshold is satisfied may be difficult to determine and often will require an analysis of the partnership or trust agreement.

Paragraph 3

Paragraph 3 provides rules that modify the maximum rates of tax at source provided in paragraph 2 in particular cases. Paragraph 3 denies the lower direct investment withholding rate of paragraph 2(a) for dividends paid by a U.S. Regulated Investment Company (RIC) or a U.S. Real Estate Investment Trust (REIT). The paragraph also denies the benefits of subparagraph (b) of paragraph 2 to dividends paid by REITs in certain circumstances, allowing them to be taxed at the U.S. statutory rate (30 percent). The United States limits the source tax on dividends paid by a REIT to the 15 percent rate when the beneficial owner of the dividend is an individual resident of the other State that owns a less than 25 percent interest in the REIT. The rules of paragraph 3 will apply to dividends paid by companies resident in Thailand that are determined by mutual agreement of the competent authorities to be similar to U.S. RIC's and REIT's.

The denial of the 10 percent withholding rate at source to all RIC and REIT shareholders, and the denial of the 15 percent rate to all but less than 25 percent individual shareholders of REITs is intended to prevent the use of these entities to gain unjustifiable source taxation benefits for certain shareholders resident in Thailand. For example, a corporation resident in Thailand that wishes to hold a diversified portfolio of U.S. corporate shares may hold the portfolio directly and pay a U.S. withholding tax of 15 percent on all of the dividends that it receives. Alternatively, it may acquire a diversified portfolio by purchasing shares representing a 10 percent or greater interest in a RIC. Since the RIC may be a pure conduit, there may be no U.S. tax costs to interposing the RIC in the chain of ownership. Absent the special rule in paragraph 2, use of the RIC could transform portfolio dividends, taxable in the United States under the Convention at 15 percent, into direct investment dividends taxable only at 10 percent.

Similarly, a resident of Thailand directly holding U.S. real property would pay U.S. tax either at a 30 percent rate on the gross income or at graduated rates on the net income. As in the preceding example, by placing the real property in a REIT, the investor could transform real estate income into dividend income, taxable at the rates provided in Article 10, significantly reducing the U.S. tax burden that otherwise would be imposed. To prevent this circumvention of U.S. rules applicable to real property, most REIT shareholders are subject to 30 percent tax at source. However, since a relatively small individual investor who might be subject to a U.S. tax of 15 percent of the net income even if he earned the real estate income directly, individuals who hold less than a 10 percent interest in the REIT remain taxable at source at a 15 percent rate.

Paragraph 4

Paragraph 4 defines the term dividends broadly and flexibly. The definition is intended to cover all arrangements that yield a return on an equity investment in a corporation as determined under the tax law of the state of source, as well as arrangements that might be developed in the future.

The term dividends includes income from shares, or other corporate rights that are not treated as debt under the law of the source State, that participate in the profits of the company. The term also includes income that is subjected to the same tax treatment as income from shares by the law of the State of source. Thus, a constructive dividend that results from a non-arm's length transaction between a corporation and a related party is a dividend. In the case of the United States the term dividend includes amounts treated as a dividend under U.S. law upon the sale or redemption of shares or upon a transfer of shares in a reorganization. See, e.g., Rev. Rul. 92-85, 1992-2 C.B. 69 (sale of foreign subsidiary's stock to U.S. sister company is a deemed dividend to extent of subsidiary's and sister's earnings and profits). Further, a distribution from a U.S. publicly traded limited partnership, which is taxed as a corporation under U.S. law, is a dividend for purposes of Article 10. However, a distribution by a limited liability company is not taxable by the United States under Article 10, provided the limited liability company is not characterized as an association taxable as a corporation under U.S. law. Finally, a payment denominated as interest that is made by a thinly capitalized corporation may be treated as a dividend to the extent that the debt is recharacterized as equity under the laws of the source State. Moreover, the term "dividends" includes income from any arrangement, including debt obligation, carrying the right to participate in profits, to the extent so characterized under the law of the Contracting State in which the income arises.

Paragraph 5

Paragraph 5 excludes from the source country limitations under paragraph 2 and paragraph 3 dividends paid with respect to holdings that form part of the business property of a permanent establishment or a fixed base. Such dividends will be taxed on a net basis using the rates and rules of taxation generally applicable to residents of the State in which the permanent establishment or fixed base is located, as modified by the Convention. An example of dividends paid with respect to the business property of a permanent establishment would be dividends derived by a dealer in stock or securities from stock or securities that the dealer held for sale to customers.

In the case of a permanent establishment or fixed base that once existed in the State but that no longer exists, the provisions of paragraph 5 also apply, by virtue of paragraph 9 of Article 7 (Business Profits), to dividends that would be attributable to such a permanent establishment or fixed base if it did exist in the year of payment or accrual. See the Technical Explanation of paragraph 9 of Article 7.

Relation to Other Articles

The branch tax rules, which are frequently dealt with in the dividends article, are dealt with in this Convention in a separate article, Article 14 (Branch Tax).

Notwithstanding the foregoing limitations on source country taxation of dividends, the saving clause of paragraph 2 of Article 1 permits the United States to tax dividends received by its residents and citizens as if the Convention had not come into effect.

The benefits of this Article are also subject to the provisions of Article 18 (Limitation on Benefits). Thus, if a resident of Thailand is the beneficial owner of dividends paid by a U.S. corporation, the shareholder must qualify for treaty benefits under at least one of the tests of Article 18 in order to receive the benefits of this Article.

Article 11 (Interest)

Article 11 provides rules for the taxation of interest paid by a resident of one Contracting State to a beneficial owner that is a resident of the other Contracting State. The Article provides for full residence country taxation of such interest and a limited source country right to tax.

Paragraph 1

Paragraph 1 preserves the right of a Contracting State to tax interest paid to its residents that arises in the other Contracting State. It does not limit the rate of tax or the manner in which it may be imposed.

Paragraph 2

Paragraph 2 allows the State where interest arises, as defined in paragraph 6, to tax the interest, except as provided in paragraph 3. If, however, the beneficial owner of the interest is a resident of the other Contracting State, the tax may not exceed the maximum rates specified in subparagraphs (a), (b) and (c). Subparagraph (a) applies to interest beneficially owned by any financial institution (including an insurance company). The rate of tax at source on such interest may not exceed 10 percent of the gross amount of the interest.

Subparagraph (b) applies to interest beneficially owned by a resident of the other Contracting State that is paid on indebtedness arising out of a sale on credit by a resident of that other State of any equipment, merchandise or services. Subparagraph (b) does not apply where the sale was between persons not dealing with each other at arm's length. Subparagraph (b) also imposes a ceiling of 10 percent of the gross amount of such interest.

Subparagraph (c) applies to all other categories of interest that are not dealt with in paragraph 3. That subparagraph imposes a ceiling of 15 percent of the gross amount of such interest.

The term "beneficial owner" is not defined in the Convention, and is, therefore, defined as under the internal law of the country imposing tax (i.e., the source country). The beneficial owner of the interest for purposes of Article 11 is the person to which the interest income is attributable for tax purposes under the laws of the source State. Thus, if interest paid by a resident of one of the States (as determined under Article 4 (Residence)) is received by a nominee or agent that is a resident of the other State on behalf of a person that is not a resident of that other State, the interest is not entitled to the benefits of this Article. However, interest received by a nominee on behalf of a resident of that other State would be entitled to benefits. Further, in accordance with paragraph 8 of the OECD Commentaries to Article 11, the source State may disregard as beneficial owner certain persons that nominally may receive interest but in substance do not control it. See also, paragraph 24 of the OECD Commentaries to Article 1 (General Scope).

Paragraph 3

As an exception to the limited, positive taxation at source under paragraph 2, paragraph 3 provides for exemption from source State taxation for interest paid to the Government of the other Contracting State and for interest paid to a resident of the other Contracting State with respect to debt obligations guaranteed or insured by the Government of that State.

Paragraph 3(a) defines the "Government of Thailand" for the purpose of this paragraph to include the Bank of Thailand, the Export-Import Bank of Thailand, the local authorities, and such financial institutions, the capital of which is wholly owned by the Government of Thailand or by any local authority, as may be agreed by the competent authorities of the Contracting States.

Paragraph 3(b) defines the Government of the United States for purposes of this paragraph to include the Federal Reserve Banks, the Export-Import Bank, the Overseas Private Investment Corporation, the states and local authorities, and such financial institutions, the capital of which is wholly owned by the Government of the United States or by any state or any local authority, as may be agreed by the competent authorities of the Contracting States.

Paragraph 4

The term "interest" is defined in paragraph 4 for purposes of Article 11. The term is defined to mean income from debt claims of every kind, whether or not secured by a mortgage. This includes income from Government securities and from bonds and debentures, and includes premiums or prizes attaching to such securities. Interest that is paid or accrued subject to a contingency is also within the ambit of Article 11. This includes income from a debt obligation carrying the right to participate in the debtor's profits. The term does not, however, include amounts, that are treated as dividends under Article 10 (Dividends).

The term interest also includes amounts subject to the same tax treatment as income from money lent under the law of the State in which the income arises. Thus, for purposes of the Convention amounts that the United States will treat as interest include (i) the difference between the issue price and the stated redemption price at maturity of a debt instrument, *i.e.*, original issue discount (OID), which may be wholly or partially realized on the disposition of a debt instrument (section 1273), (ii) amounts that are imputed interest on a deferred sales contract (section 483), (iii) amounts treated as OID under the stripped bond rules (section 1286), (iv) amounts treated as original issue discount under the below-market interest rate rules (section 7872), (v) a partner's distributive share of a partnership's interest income (section 702), (vi) the interest portion of periodic payments made under a "finance lease" or similar contractual arrangement that in substance is a borrowing by the nominal lessee to finance the acquisition of property, (vii) amounts included in the income of a holder of a residual interest in a REMIC (section 860E), because these amounts generally are subject to the same taxation treatment as interest under U.S. tax law, and (viii) imbedded interest with respect to notional principal contracts.

Paragraph 5

Paragraph 5 provides an exception to the rules of paragraphs 2 and 3 that limit the rate of source country taxation of interest. This paragraph applies in cases where the beneficial owner of the interest carries on business through a permanent establishment in the State of source or performs independent personal services from a fixed base situated in that State and the interest is - effectively connected with that permanent establishment or fixed base, or with activities referred to in subparagraphs (b) and (c) of paragraph 1 of Article 7 (Business Profits) (i.e., income from activities similar to those carried on through the permanent establishment, but not carried on through the permanent establishment for tax avoidance reasons). In these cases the provisions of Article 7 (Business Profits) or Article 15 (Independent Personal Services) will apply and the State of source will retain the right to impose tax on such interest income, consistent with the rules of those Articles.

In the case of a permanent establishment or fixed base that once existed in the State but that no longer exists, the provisions of paragraph 5 also apply, by virtue of paragraph 9 of Article 7 (Business Profits), to interest that would be attributable to such a permanent establishment or fixed base if it did exist in the year of payment or accrual. See the Technical Explanation of paragraph 9 of Article 7.

Paragraph 6

Paragraph 6 provides rules for sourcing interest. Generally, interest is deemed to arise in a Contracting State when the payer is the State itself, a political subdivision, a local authority or a resident of that State. When the payer has a permanent establishment or fixed base in a Contracting State in connection with which the indebtedness on which the interest is paid was incurred and the interest is borne by the permanent establishment or fixed base, then the interest is deemed to arise in the State where the permanent establishment or fixed base is located. This rule applies whether or not the payer is a resident of a Contracting State.

Paragraph 7

Paragraph 7 provides that in cases involving special relationships between persons, Article 11 applies only to that portion of the total interest payments that would have been made absent such special relationships (i.e., an arm's-length interest payment). Any excess amount of interest paid remains taxable according to the laws of the United States and Thailand, respectively, with due regard to the other provisions of the Convention. Thus, if the excess amount would be treated under the source country's law as a distribution of profits by a corporation, such amount could be taxed as a dividend rather than as interest, but the tax would be subject, if appropriate, to the rate limitations of paragraph 2 of Article 10 (Dividends).

The term "special relationship" is not defined in the Convention. In applying this paragraph the United States considers the term to include the relationships described in Article 9, which in turn corresponds to the definition of "control" for purposes of section 482 of the Code.

This paragraph does not address cases where, owing to a special relationship between the payer and the beneficial owner or between both of them and some other person, the amount of the interest is less than an arm's-length amount. In those cases a transaction may be characterized to reflect its substance and interest may be imputed consistent with the definition of interest in paragraph 4. The United States would apply section 482 or 7872 of the Code to determine the amount of imputed interest in those cases.

Paragraph 8

Paragraph 8 provides an anti-abuse exception to the reduced source-country taxation provided for in paragraphs 2 and 3. This exception is consistent with the policy of Code sections 860E(e) and 860G(b) that excess inclusions with respect to a real estate mortgage investment conduit (REMIC) should bear full U.S. tax in all cases. Without a full tax at source foreign purchasers of residual interests would have a competitive advantage over U.S. purchasers at the time these interests are initially offered. Also, absent this rule the U.S. fisc would suffer a revenue loss with respect to mortgages held in a REMIC because of opportunities for tax avoidance created by differences in the timing of taxable and economic income produced by these interests.

Relation to Other Articles

Notwithstanding the limitations on source country taxation of interest in this Article, the saving clause of paragraph 2 of Article 1 permits the United States to tax its residents and citizens as if the Convention had not come into force. Thus, a U.S. citizen living in Thailand who receives U.S.-source interest includes that income in his worldwide income that is subject to U.S. tax at ordinary rates.

As with other benefits of the Convention, the benefits of reduced source-State taxation, or source-State exemption, under paragraphs 2 and 3 of this Article, are available to a resident of the other State only if that resident is entitled to those benefits under the provisions of Article 18 (Limitation on Benefits).

Article 12 (Royalties)

Article 12 provides rules for the taxation of royalties paid by a resident of one Contracting State to a beneficial owner that is a resident of the other Contracting State. The Article provides for full residence country taxation of such royalties and a limited source country right to tax.

Paragraph 1

Paragraph 1 preserves the right of a Contracting State to tax royalties paid to its residents and arising in the other Contracting State, subject to exceptions provided in paragraph 4 (for royalties taxable as business profits and independent personal services).

Paragraphs 2 and 3

Paragraph 2 allows the state of source to tax royalties. If, however, the beneficial owner of the royalty payment is a resident of the other Contracting State, the tax may not exceed the ceilings stated in subparagraphs (a), (b) and (c) for the different classes of royalties described in paragraph 3. Paragraph 3 defines the term "royalties" for purposes of Article 12.

Subparagraph (a) of paragraph 2 applies to the classes of royalties described in subparagraph (a) of paragraph 3. These are royalties paid for the use of or the right to use copyrights of literary, artistic or scientific work, including software, and motion pictures and works on film, tape or other means of reproduction for radio or television broadcasting. Subparagraph (a) of paragraph 2 limits the tax that may be imposed by the source country on such royalties to a maximum rate of 5 percent of the gross amount of the royalties.

Computer software generally is protected by copyright laws around the world. Under the Convention consideration received for the use or the right to use computer software is treated either as royalties or as income from the alienation of tangible personal property, depending on the facts and circumstances of the transaction giving rise to the payment. It is also understood that payments received in connection with the transfer of so-called "shrink-wrap" computer software are treated as business profits.

Consideration for the use or right to use works on film, tape or other means of reproduction for use in connection with radio or television broadcasting is specifically included in the definition of royalties. It is intended that subsequent technological advances in the field of radio and television broadcasting will not affect the inclusion of payments relating to use of such means of reproduction in the definition of royalties.

It is also understood that if an artist who is resident in one Contracting State records a performance in the other Contracting State, retains a copyrighted interest in a recording, and receives payments for the right to use the recording based on the sale or public playing of the recording, then the right of such other Contracting State to tax those payments is governed by Article 12. See Boulez v. Commissioner, 83 T.C. 584 (1984), aff'd, 810 F.2d 209 (D.C. Cir. 1986).

Subparagraph (b) of paragraph 2 applies to royalties described in subparagraph (b) of paragraph 3. These are royalties paid for the use of or the right to use industrial, commercial or scientific equipment. Subparagraph (b) of paragraph 2 limits the source-country tax that may be imposed on such royalties to 8 percent of the gross amount of the royalty. In the U.S. Model and in most U.S. treaties such income is treated as business profits, and not as royalties. Thailand's treaty policy is to include such income within the scope of the royalties article and tax the income as an industrial royalty. The Convention includes the income within the scope of Article 12, but applies a rate lower than that applicable to industrial royalties.

Subparagraph (c) of paragraph 2 applies to royalties described in subparagraph (c) of paragraph 3. The royalties that fall into this category are payments for the use of or the right to use any patent, trademark, design or model, plan, secret formula or process, or for information concerning industrial, commercial or scientific experience. The source-country tax imposed on such royalties by subparagraph (c) of paragraph 2 may not exceed 15 percent of such royalties.

The term "industrial, commercial, or scientific experience" (sometimes referred to as "know-how") has the meaning ascribed to it in paragraph 11 of the Commentary to Article 12 of the OECD Model Convention. Consistent with that meaning, the term may include information that is ancillary to a right otherwise giving rise to royalties, such as a patent or secret process.

Know-how also may include, in limited cases, technical information that is conveyed through technical or consultancy services. It does not include general educational training of the user's employees, nor does it include information developed especially for the user, for example, a technical plan or design developed according to the user's specifications. Thus, as provided in paragraph 11 of the Commentaries to Article 12 of the OECD Model, the term "royalties" does not include payments received as consideration for after-sales service, for services rendered by a seller to a purchaser under a guarantee, or for pure technical assistance.

The term "royalties" as used in all three subparagraphs of these paragraphs includes gain derived from the alienation of any right or property that would give rise to royalties, to the extent the gain is contingent on the productivity, use, or further alienation thereof. Gains that are not so contingent are dealt with under Article 13 (Gains).

The term "royalties" is defined in the Convention and therefore is generally independent of domestic law. Certain terms used in the definition are not defined in the Convention, but these may be defined under domestic tax law. For example, the term "secret process or formulas" is found in the Code, and its meaning has been elaborated in the context of sections 351 and 367. See Rev. Rul. 55-17, 1955-1 C.B. 388; Rev. Rul. 64-56, 1964-1 C.B. 133; Rev. Proc. 69-19, 1969-2 C.B. 301.

The term "royalties" does not include payments for professional services (such as architectural, engineering, legal, managerial, medical and software development services). For example, income from the design of a refinery by an engineer (even if the engineer employed know-how in the process of rendering the design) or the production of a legal brief by a lawyer is not income from the transfer of know-how taxable under Article 12, but is income from services taxable under either Article 15 (Independent Personal Services) or Article 16 (Dependent Personal Services). Professional services may be embodied in property that gives rise to royalties, however. Thus, if a professional contracts to develop patentable property and retains rights in the resulting property under the development contract, subsequent license payments made for those rights would be royalties.

The term "beneficial owner" is not defined in the Convention, and is, therefore, defined as under the internal law of the country imposing tax (i.e., the source country). The beneficial owner of a royalty for purposes of Article 12 is the person to which the royalty income is attributable for tax purposes under the laws of the source State. Thus, if a royalty paid by a resident of one of the States (as determined under Article 4 (Residence)) is received by a nominee or agent that is a resident of the other State on behalf of a person that is not a resident of that other State, the royalty is not entitled to the benefits of this Article. However, a royalty received by a nominee on behalf of a resident of that other State would be entitled to benefits. Further, in accordance with paragraph 4 of the OECD Commentaries to Article 12, the source State may disregard as beneficial owner certain persons that nominally may receive a royalty but in substance do not control it. See also, paragraph 24 of the OECD Commentaries to Article 1 (General Scope).

Paragraph 4

Paragraph 4 provides an exception to the rules of paragraph 2 that limit the rate of source country taxation of royalties. This paragraph applies in cases where the beneficial owner of the royalties carries on business through a permanent establishment in the State of source or performs independent personal services from a fixed base situated in that State and the royalties are effectively connected with that permanent establishment or fixed base, or with activities referred to in subparagraph (c) of paragraph 1 of Article 7 (Business Profits) (i.e., activities similar to those carried on through the permanent establishment, but not carried on through the permanent establishment for tax avoidance reasons). In these cases the provisions of Article 7 (Business Profits) or Article 15 (Independent Personal Services) will apply and the State of source will retain the right to impose tax on such royalty income, consistent with the rules of those Articles.

In the case of a permanent establishment or fixed base that once existed in the State but that no longer exists, the provisions of paragraph 4 also apply, by virtue of paragraph 9 of Article 7 (Business Profits), to royalties that would be attributable to such a permanent establishment or fixed base if it did exist in the year of payment or accrual. See the Technical Explanation of paragraph 9 of Article 7.

Paragraph 5

Paragraph 5 provides rules for sourcing royalty payments. Under paragraph 5 (a), royalty payments are deemed to arise in a Contracting State when the payer is that State itself, a political subdivision, a local authority or a resident of that State. However, when the person paying the royalty has a permanent establishment or fixed base in a Contracting State in connection with which the liability to pay the royalty was incurred and the royalty is borne by the permanent establishment or fixed base, then the royalty is deemed to arise in the Contracting State in which the permanent establishment or fixed base is located. This rule applies whether or not the payer is a resident of a Contracting State. Under paragraph 5 (b), in cases where paragraph 5 (a) does not operate to deem the royalty to arise in one of the Contracting States, and the royalty relates to the use or right to use any property or rights described in paragraph 3 in one of the Contracting States, then the royalty is deemed to arise in that State.

Paragraph 6

Paragraph 6 provides that in cases involving special relationships between the payor and beneficial owner of royalties, Article 12 applies only to the extent the royalties would have been paid absent such special relationships (i.e., an arm's-length royalty). Any excess amount of royalties paid remains taxable according to the laws of the two Contracting States with due regard to the other provisions of the Convention. If, for example, the excess amount is treated as a distribution of corporate profits under domestic law, such excess amount will be taxed as a dividend rather than as royalties, but the tax imposed on the dividend payment will be subject to the rate limitations of paragraph 2 of Article 10 (Dividends).

Relation to Other Articles

Notwithstanding the foregoing limitations on source country taxation of royalties, the saving clause of paragraph 2 of Article 1 (Personal Scope) permits the United States to tax its residents and citizens as if the Convention had not come into force.

As with other benefits of the Convention, the benefit of limited source State taxation of royalties under paragraph 2 of Article 12 is available to a resident of the other State only if that resident is entitled to those benefits under Article 18 (Limitation on Benefits).

Article 13 (Gains)

Paragraph 1

Paragraph 1 of Article 13 preserves for both Contracting States the non-exclusive right to tax gains attributable to the alienation of property in accordance with its domestic law. The paragraph therefore permits the United States to apply section 897 of the Code to tax gains derived by a resident of the other Contracting State that are attributable to the alienation of real property situated in the United States (as defined in paragraph 2). Gains attributable to the alienation of real property include gain from any other property that is treated as a real property interest. This includes real property referred to in Article 6 (i.e., an interest in the real property itself), a "United States real property interest" (when the United States is the other Contracting State under paragraph 1), and an equivalent interest in real property situated in Thailand. Under section 897(c) of the Code the term "United States real property interest" includes shares in a U.S. corporation that owns sufficient U.S. real property interests to satisfy an asset-ratio test on certain testing dates. The term also includes certain foreign corporations that have elected to be treated as U.S. corporations for this purpose. Section 897(i). In applying paragraph 1 the United States will look through distributions made by a REIT. Accordingly, distributions made by a REIT are taxable under paragraph 1 of Article 13 (not under Article 10 (Dividends)) when they are attributable to gains derived from the alienation of real property. Furthermore, both the residence state and the source state under the domestic law of each may tax gains from the alienation of movable property forming part of the business property of a permanent establishment that an enterprise of a Contracting State has in the other Contracting State or of movable property pertaining to a fixed base available to a resident of a Contracting State in the other Contracting State for the purpose of performing independent personal services. This also includes gains from the alienation of such a permanent establishment (alone or with the whole enterprise) or of such fixed base.

A resident of Thailand that is a partner in a partnership doing business in the United States generally will have a permanent establishment in the United States as a result of the activities of the partnership, assuming that the activities of the partnership rise to the level of a permanent establishment. Rev. Rul. 91-32, 1991-1 C.B. 107. Further, the United States generally may tax a partner's distributive share of income realized by a partnership on the disposition of movable property forming part of the business property of the partnership.

Paragraph 2

Paragraph 2 grants exclusive taxing jurisdiction to the state of residence of the alienator with respect to gains from the alienation of ships, aircraft, or containers operated in international traffic or movable property pertaining to the operation of such ships, aircraft, or containers. Under paragraph 2 when such income is derived by an enterprise of a Contracting State it is taxable only in that Contracting State. The rules of this paragraph apply even if the income is attributable to a permanent establishment maintained by the enterprise in the other Contracting State. This result is generally consistent with Article 8 (Shipping and Air Transport), which confers exclusive taxing rights over international air transport income on the state of residence of the enterprise deriving such income.

Article 14 (Branch Tax)

Paragraph 1

Paragraph 1 permits a Contracting State to impose tax on a corporation resident in the other Contracting State in addition to the taxes that may be imposed under the other provisions of the Convention. The scope of the taxes that may be imposed under this paragraph is specified in paragraph 2 for the United States, and in paragraph 3 for Thailand. The rates are specified in paragraph 4. Since the term "corporation" is not defined in the Convention, it will be defined for this purpose under the law of State imposing the tax.

Paragraph 2

Paragraph 2 describes the branch taxes that the United States may impose. Subparagraph (a) deals with the U.S. branch profits tax. Under this subparagraph the U.S. branch profits tax may be imposed on the "dividend equivalent amount" of the income of a corporation resident in Thailand to the extent of the corporation's business profits that are effectively connected (or treated as effectively connected) with the conduct of a trade or business in the United States and which meet one of three additional tests: (1) they are attributable to a permanent establishment in the United States; (2) the income is subject to tax under Article 6 (Income from Immovable (Real) Property); or (3) the income is in the form of a gain subject to tax under Article 13. The United States may not impose its branch profits tax on the business profits of a corporation resident in Thailand that are effectively connected with a U.S. trade or business but that are not attributable to a permanent establishment or are not otherwise subject to U.S. taxation under Article 6 or - Article 13 (Gains).

The term "dividend equivalent amount" used in paragraph 2 has the same meaning that it has under section 884 of the Code, as amended from time to time, provided the amendments are consistent with the purpose of the branch profits tax. Generally, the dividend equivalent amount for a particular year is the income described above that is included in the corporation's effectively connected earnings and profits for that year, after payment of the corporate tax under Articles 6, 7 or 13, reduced for any increase in the branch's U.S. net equity during the year and increased for any reduction in its U.S. net equity during the year. U.S. net equity is U.S. assets less U.S. liabilities. See, Treas. Reg. section 1.884-1. The dividend equivalent amount for any year approximates the dividend that a U.S. branch office would have paid during the year if the branch had been operated as a separate U.S. subsidiary company.

Paragraph 2(b) permits the United States to impose its branch excess interest tax on a corporation resident in Thailand. The base of this tax is the excess, if any, of the interest deductible in the United States in computing the profits of the corporation that are subject to tax in the United States and are either attributable to a permanent establishment in the United States or subject to tax in the United States under Article 6 or Article 13 of this Convention over the interest paid by or from the permanent establishment or trade or business in the United States.

Paragraph 3

Paragraph 3 deals with the Thai tax referred to in paragraph 1. Under this provision, a company resident in the United States may be subject to a tax, in addition to the other taxes allowed under this Convention (e.g.,the tax on business profits under Article 7), on the disposal of profits out of Thailand. Any tax imposed under this provision must be consistent with the provisions of Thai law. The Thai tax, imposed under section 70 bis of the Thai tax law, is charged on the portion of the profits of a Thai branch of a foreign corporation, after the normal corporate tax, that is remitted to the foreign head office.

Paragraph 4

Paragraph 4 specifies the rates at which the taxes described in paragraphs 2 and 3 may be imposed. Paragraph 4 (a) provides that the branch profits taxes described in paragraphs 2(a), for the United States, and 3, for Thailand, shall not be imposed at a rate exceeding the direct investment dividend withholding rate of 10 percent, as provided in paragraph 2(a) of Article 10 (Dividends).

Paragraph 4(b) provides that the U.S. branch excess interest tax described in paragraph 2(b) shall not be imposed at a rate exceeding the appropriate rate specified in paragraph 2 of Article 11 (Interest). Since the excess interest tax is treated as though it is imposed on interest payments from a U.S. subsidiary to its foreign parent corporation, the rate at which the tax is imposed will depend on the nature of the business in which the "parent" (i.e., the home office) is engaged. Thus, for example, if the enterprise is a bank, the excess interest tax would be imposed at a 10 percent rate, since that is the rate under Article 11 for interest beneficially owned by financial institutions. For most other types of enterprises, the branch excess interest tax would be imposed at the 15 percent rate.

Relation to Other Articles

As with other benefits of the Convention, the benefits of reduced rates of branch tax under this Article are available to a resident of the other State only if that resident is entitled to those benefits under the provisions of Article 18 (Limitation on Benefits).

Article 15 (Independent Personal Services)

The Convention deals in separate articles with different classes of income from personal services. Article 15 deals with the general class of income from independent personal services and Article 16 deals with the general class of income from dependent personal services. Articles 17 and 19 through 23 provide exceptions and additions to these general rules for directors' fees (Article 17); performance income of artistes and sportsmen (Article 19); pensions in respect of personal service income, social security benefits, annuities, alimony, and child support payments (Article 20); government service salaries and pensions (Article 21); certain income of students and trainees (Article 22); and certain income of teachers or researchers (Article 23).

Paragraph 1

Paragraph 1 of Article 15 provides the general rule that an individual who is a resident of a Contracting State and who derives income from performing professional services or other activities of an independent character will be exempt from tax in respect of that income by the other Contracting State, unless the conditions specified in any of subparagraphs (a), (b) or (c) are met. If one of these three circumstances are met, such income will also be subject to tax by the other Contracting State (i.e., the host State).

Under subparagraph (a), the income may be taxed by the host State if there is a fixed base regularly available to the individual for the purposes of performing his services. In that case, the host State may tax that portion of the income that is attributable to a fixed base. Unlike the U.S. Model, and most U.S. treaties, this Convention does not require that the services be performed in the host State to be taxable there, only that they be attributable to a fixed base located there.

The term "fixed base" is not defined in the Convention, but its meaning is understood to be similar, but not identical, to that of the term "permanent establishment," as defined in Article 5 (Permanent Establishment). The term "regularly available" also is not defined in the Convention. Whether a fixed base is regularly available to a person will be determined based on all the facts and circumstances. In general, the term encompasses situations where a fixed base is at the disposal of the individual whenever he performs services in that State. It is not necessary that the individual regularly use the fixed base, only that the fixed base be regularly available to him. For example, a U.S. resident partner in a law firm that has offices in Thailand would be considered to have a fixed base regularly available to him in Thailand if the law firm had an office in Thailand that was available to him whenever he wished to conduct business in Thailand, regardless of how frequently he conducted business in Thailand, or in that office. On the other hand, an individual who had no office in Thailand and occasionally rented a hotel room to serve as a temporary office would not be considered to have a fixed base regularly available to him.

It is not necessary that the individual actually use the fixed base. It is only necessary that the fixed base be regularly available to him. For example, if an individual has an office in the other State, that fixed base will be considered to be regularly available to him regardless of whether he conducts his activities there.

Because of the absence of a "place of performance" test in this Article, if, for example, an American lawyer who has an office available to him in Bangkok visits Bangkok to work on a case, and the case requires him to spend some work time in Vietnam, the income from the services performed in Vietnam, since they are part of the services being carried on through the Bangkok law office, would be attributable to that fixed base.

Under paragraph 1(b), the income may be taxed in the host State if the individual's stay in that State is for a period or periods aggregating 90 days or more during the fiscal year. If that time threshold is met, only the income that is derived from his activities performed in that State may be taxed there. This rule is consistent with the provisions of paragraph 3(b) of Article 5 (Permanent Establishment), under which the furnishing of services by an enterprise constitutes a permanent establishment if the activities continue for a period of 90 days or more in a 12-month period.

Under paragraph 1(c), the income may be taxed in the host State if the remuneration for the individual's activities is paid by a resident of that other State or borne by a permanent establishment or fixed base situated in that other State and the remuneration exceeds in that fiscal year 10,000 United States dollars or its equivalent in Thai currency. This dollar threshold does not include expenses reimbursed to the individual or borne on his behalf.

Although, unlike the U.S. Model, this Article does not specify that the income subject to tax under this article is to be taxed on a net basis, it is understood that the principles of paragraph 3 of Article 7 (Business profits) should be applied in computing the individual's income for purposes of taxation under this Article.

Income derived by persons other than individuals or groups of individuals from the performance of independent personal services is not covered by Article 15. Such income generally would be business profits taxable in accordance with Article 7 (Business Profits). Income derived by employees of such persons generally would be taxable in accordance with Article 16 (Dependent Personal Services).

This Article applies to income derived by a partner resident in the Contracting State that is attributable to personal services of an independent character performed in the other State through a partnership that has a fixed base in that other Contracting State. Income which may be taxed under this Article includes all income attributable to the fixed base in respect of the performance of the personal services carried on by the partnership (whether by the partner himself, other partners in the partnership, or by employees assisting the partners) and any income from activities ancillary to the performance of those services (for example, charges for facsimile services). Income that is not derived from the performance of personal services and that is not ancillary thereto (for example, rental income from subletting office space), will be governed by other Articles of the Convention.

The application paragraph 1(a) of Article 15 to a service partnership may be illustrated by the following example: a partnership formed in the U.S. has five partners (who agree to split profits equally), four of whom are resident and perform personal services only in the U.S. at Office A, and one of whom performs personal services from Office B, a fixed base in Thailand. In this case, the four partners of the partnership resident in the U.S. may be taxed in Thailand in respect of their share of the income attributable to the fixed base, Office B. The services giving rise to income which may be attributed to the fixed base would include not only the services performed by the one resident partner, but also, for example, if one of the four other partners went to Thailand and worked on an Office B matter there, the income in respect of those services. As noted above in the discussion of the term "regularly available", this would be the case regardless of whether the partner from the U.S. actually visited or used Office B when performing services in Thailand.

Paragraph 9 of Article 7 (Business Profits) refers to paragraph 1(a) of Article 15. That rule clarifies that income that is attributable to a permanent establishment or a fixed base, but that is deferred and received after the permanent establishment or fixed base no longer exists, may nevertheless be taxed by the State in which the permanent establishment or fixed base was located. Thus, under Article 15, income derived by an individual resident of a Contracting State from services performed in the other Contracting State and attributable to a fixed base there may be taxed by that other State even if the income is deferred and received after there is no longer a fixed base available to the resident in that other State.

Paragraph 2

Paragraph 2 notes that the term "professional services" includes scientific, literary, artistic, educational or teaching activities as well as the independent activities of physicians, lawyers, engineers, architects, dentists, and accountants. This list, which is derived from the OECD Model, is not exhaustive. The term includes all personal services performed by an individual for his own account, where he receives the income and bears the risk of loss arising from the services. However, the taxation of income from types of independent services that are covered by Articles 17 and 19 through 23 are governed by the provisions of those articles.

Relation to Other Articles

If an individual resident of Thailand who is also a U.S. citizen performs professional services or other independent activities in the United States, the United States may, by virtue of the saving clause of paragraph 2 of Article 1 (Personal Scope) tax his income without regard to the restrictions of this Article.

Article 16 (Dependent Personal Services)

Article 16 apportions taxing jurisdiction over remuneration derived by a resident of a Contracting State as an employee between the States of source and residence.

Paragraph 1

The general rule of Article 16 is contained in paragraph 1. Remuneration derived by a resident of a Contracting State as an employee may be taxed by the State of residence, and the remuneration also may be taxed by that other Contracting State to the extent derived from employment exercised (i.e., services performed) in the other Contracting State. Paragraph 1 also provides that the more specific rules of Articles 17 (Directors' Fees), 20 (Pensions and Social Security Payments), 21 (Government Service), 22 (Students and Trainees) and 23 (Teachers) apply in the case of employment income described in one of these articles. Thus, even though the State of source has a right to tax employment income under Article 16, it may not have the right to tax that income under the Convention if the income is described, e.g., in Article 20 (Pensions, Social Security, Annuities, Alimony and Child Support) and is not taxable in the State of source under the provisions of that article.

Article 16 applies to "salaries, wages and other similar remuneration." The U.S. Model has deleted the term "similar." Even with the inclusion of the term "similar," Article 16 should be understood to apply to any form of compensation for employment, including payments in kind, regardless of whether the remuneration could be characterized as salaries and wages.

Consistently with section 864(c)(6), Article 16 also applies regardless of the timing of actual payment for services. Thus, a bonus paid to a resident of a Contracting State with respect to services performed in the other Contracting State with respect to a particular taxable year would be subject to Article 16 for that year even if it was paid after the close of the year. Similarly, an annuity received for services performed in a taxable year would be subject to Article

16 despite the fact that it was paid in subsequent years. In either case, whether such payments were taxable in the State where the employment was exercised would depend on whether the tests of paragraph 2 were satisfied. Consequently, a person who receives the right to a future payment in consideration for services rendered in a Contracting State would be taxable in that State even if the payment is received at a time when the recipient is a resident of the other Contracting State.

Paragraph 2

Paragraph 2 sets forth an exception to the general rule that employment income may be taxed in the State where it is exercised. Under paragraph 2, the State where the employment is exercised may not tax the income from the employment if three conditions are satisfied: (a) the individual is present in the other Contracting State for a period or periods not exceeding 183 days in any 12-month period that begins or ends during the relevant (i.e., the year in which the services are performed) calendar year; (b) the remuneration is paid by, or on behalf of, an employer who is not a resident of that other Contracting State; and (c) the remuneration is not borne as a deductible expense by a permanent establishment or fixed base that the employer has in that other State. In order for the remuneration to be exempt from tax in the source State, all three conditions must be satisfied. This exception is identical to those set forth in the OECD and U.S. Models.

The 183-day period in condition (a) is to be measured using the "days of physical presence" method. Under this method, the days that are counted include any day in which a part of the day is spent in the host country. (Rev. Rul. 56-24, 1956-1 C.B. 851.) Thus, days that are counted include the days of arrival and departure; weekends and holidays on which the employee does not work but is present within the country; vacation days spent in the country before, during or after the employment period, unless the individual's presence before or after the employment can be shown to be independent of his presence there for employment purposes; and time during periods of sickness, training periods, strikes, etc., when the individual is present but not working. If illness prevented the individual from leaving the country in sufficient time to qualify for the benefit, those days will not count. Also, any part of a day spent in the host country while in transit between two points outside the host country is not counted. These rules are consistent with the description of the 183-day period in paragraph 5 of the Commentary to Article 15 in the OECD Model.

Conditions (b) and (c) are intended to ensure that a Contracting State will not be required to allow a deduction to the payor for compensation paid and at the same time to exempt the employee on the amount received. Accordingly, if a foreign person pays the salary of an employee who is employed in the host State, but a host State corporation or permanent establishment reimburses the payor with a payment that can be identified as a reimbursement, neither condition (b) nor (c), as the case may be, will be considered to have been fulfilled.

The reference to remuneration "borne by" a permanent establishment or fixed base is understood to encompass all expenses that economically are incurred and not merely expenses that are currently deductible for tax purposes. Accordingly, the expenses referred to include expenses that are capitalizable as well as those that are currently deductible. Further, salaries paid by residents that are exempt from income taxation may be considered to be borne by a permanent establishment or fixed base notwithstanding the fact that the expenses will be neither deductible nor capitalizable since the payor is exempt from tax.

Paragraph 3

Paragraph 3 contains a special rule applicable to remuneration for services performed by an individual resident of one Contracting State as an employee aboard a ship or aircraft operated in international traffic. Under this paragraph, the employment income of such persons may be taxed in the State of residence of the enterprise operating the ship or aircraft. This is not an exclusive taxing right. The State of residence of the employee may also tax the remuneration. This provision is based on the OECD Model. The United States Model does not contain this rule, because U.S. internal law does not impose tax on non-U.S. source income of a person who is neither a U.S. citizen nor a U.S. resident, even if that person is an employee of a U.S. resident enterprise. Thus, the United States may not tax the salary of a resident of Thailand who is employed by a U.S. carrier, except as provided in paragraph 2.

Relation to Other Articles

If a U.S. citizen who is resident in Thailand performs services as an employee in the United States and meets the conditions of paragraph 2 for source country exemption, he nevertheless is taxable in the United States by virtue of the saving clause of paragraph 2 of Article 1 (Personal Scope).

Article 17 (Directors' Fees)

This Article provides that a Contracting State may tax the fees and other compensation paid by a company that is a resident of that State for services performed outside of the other State by a resident of the other Contracting State in his capacity as a director of the company. This rule is an exception to the more general rules of Article 15 (Independent Personal Services) and Article 16 (Dependent Personal Services). Thus, for example, in determining whether a director's fee paid to a non-employee director is subject to tax in the country of residence of the corporation, it is not relevant to establish whether the fee is attributable to a fixed base in that State. The Article deals with the compensation both of directors themselves and of designees of a director who are serving in the capacity of a director.

The analogous OECD and U.S. Model provisions reach different results in certain cases. Under the OECD Model provision, a resident of one Contracting State who is a director of a corporation that is resident in the other Contracting State is subject to tax in that other State in respect of his directors' fees regardless of where the services are performed. Under the U.S.

Model, a resident of one Contracting State who is a director of a corporation that is resident in the other Contracting State is subject to tax in that other State in respect of this directors' fees only for services performed in that State. Article 17 represents a compromise between the U.S. position and the OECD Model. Under Article 17, the State of residence of the corporation may tax nonresident directors with no time or dollar threshold, but only with respect to remuneration for services that are not performed in the other State.

This Article is subject to the saving clause of paragraph 2 of Article 1 (Personal Scope). Thus, if a U.S. citizen who is a resident of Thailand is a director of a U.S. corporation, the United States may tax his full remuneration regardless of where he performs his services.

Article 18 (Limitation on Benefits)

Purpose of Limitation on Benefits Provisions

The United States views an income tax treaty as a vehicle for providing treaty benefits to residents of the two Contracting States. This statement begs the question of who is to be treated as a resident of a Contracting State for the purpose of being granted treaty benefits. The Commentaries to the OECD Model authorize a tax authority to deny benefits, under substance-over-form principles, to a nominee in one State deriving income from the other on behalf of a third-country resident. In addition, although the text of the OECD Model does not contain express anti-abuse provisions, the Commentaries to Article 1 contain an extensive discussion approving the use of such provisions in tax treaties in order to limit the ability of third state residents to obtain treaty benefits. The United States holds strongly to the view that tax treaties should include provisions that specifically prevent misuse of treaties by residents of third countries. Consequently, all recent U.S. income tax treaties contain comprehensive Limitation on Benefits provisions.

A treaty that provides treaty benefits to any resident of a Contracting State permits "treaty shopping": the use, by residents of third states, of legal entities established in a Contracting State with a principal purpose to obtain the benefits of a tax treaty between the United States and the other Contracting State. It is important to note that this definition of treaty shopping does not encompass every case in which a third state resident establishes an entity in a U.S. treaty partner, and that entity enjoys treaty benefits to which the third state resident would not itself be entitled. If the third country resident had substantial reasons for establishing the structure that were unrelated to obtaining treaty benefits, the structure would not fall within the definition of treaty shopping set forth above.

Of course, the fundamental problem presented by this approach is that it is based on the taxpayer's intent, which a tax administration is normally ill-equipped to identify. In order to avoid the necessity of making this subjective determination, Article 18 sets forth a series of objective tests. The assumption underlying each of these tests is that a taxpayer that satisfies the requirements of any of the tests probably has a real business purpose for the structure it has adopted, or has a sufficiently strong nexus to Thailand (e.g., a resident individual) to warrant benefits even in the absence of a business connection, and that this business purpose or connection outweighs any purpose to obtain the benefits of the Treaty.

For instance, the assumption underlying the active trade or business test under paragraph 2 is that a third country resident that establishes a "substantial" operation in Thailand and that derives income from a similar activity in the United States would not do so primarily to avail itself of the benefits of the Treaty; it is presumed in such a case that the investor had a valid business purpose for investing in Thailand, and that the link between that trade or business and the U.S. activity that generates the treaty-benefitted income manifests a business purpose for placing the U.S. investments in the entity in Thailand. It is considered unlikely that the investor would incur the expense of establishing a substantial trade or business in Thailand simply to obtain the benefits of the Convention. A similar rationale underlies the other tests in Article 18.

While these tests provide useful surrogates for identifying actual intent, these mechanical tests cannot account for every case in which the taxpayer was not treaty shopping. Accordingly, Article 18 also includes a provision (paragraph 4) authorizing the competent authority of a Contracting State to grant benefits. While an analysis under paragraph 4 may well differ from that under one of the other tests of Article 18, its objective is the same: to identify investors whose residence in the other State can be justified by factors other than a purpose to derive treaty benefits.

Article 18 and the anti-abuse provisions of domestic law complement each other, as Article 18 effectively determines whether an entity has a sufficient nexus to the Contracting State to be treated as a resident for treaty purposes, while domestic anti-abuse provisions (e.g., business purpose, substance-over-form, step transaction or conduit principles) determine whether a particular transaction should be recast in accordance with its substance. Thus, internal law principles of the source State may be applied to identify the beneficial owner of an item of income, and Article 18 then will be applied to the beneficial owner to determine if that person is entitled to the benefits of the Convention with respect to such income.

Structure of the Article

Article 18 follows the form used in other recent U.S. income tax treaties. The structure of the Article is as follows: Paragraph 1 states the general rule that residents are entitled to benefits otherwise accorded to residents only to the extent provided in the Article and lists a series of attributes of a resident of a Contracting State, the presence of any one of which will entitle that person to all the benefits of the Convention. Paragraph 2 provides that, with respect to a person not entitled to benefits under paragraph 1, benefits nonetheless may be granted to that person with regard to certain types of income. Paragraph 3 states that a resident of Thailand that is an "international banking facility", as defined under Thai law, is not entitled to U.S. benefits under the Convention with respect to income received from the United States. Paragraph 4 provides that benefits also may be granted if the competent authority of the State from which benefits are claimed determines that it is appropriate to provide benefits in that case. Paragraph 5 defines the term "recognized stock exchange" as used in paragraph 1(d). Paragraph 6 limits the relief allowed under the Convention for remittance taxes. Paragraph 7 provides that the competent authorities will exchange information necessary to carry out the provisions of the Article.

Paragraph 1

Paragraph 1 provides that a resident of a Contracting State deriving income from the other Contracting State will be entitled in that other Contracting State to all benefits of the Convention only if such person is described in paragraph 1. Some provisions of the Convention do not require that a person be a resident in order to enjoy the benefits of those provisions. These include paragraph 1 of Article 25 (Non-Discrimination), Article 27 (Mutual Agreement Procedure), and Article 29 (Diplomatic Agents and Consular Officers). It is to be understood that Article 22 does not limit the availability of the benefits of these provisions.

Paragraph 1 has six subparagraphs, each of which describes a category of residents that are entitled to all benefits of the Convention.

Individuals -- Subparagraph 1(a)

Subparagraph (a) provides that individual residents of a Contracting State will be entitled to all treaty benefits. If such an individual receives income as a nominee on behalf of a third-country resident, benefits may be denied under the respective articles of the Convention by the requirement that the beneficial owner of the income be a resident of a Contracting State.

Governmental Entities -- Subparagraph 1(b)

Subparagraph (b) provides that a Contracting State or a political subdivision or local authority thereof, which are all treated as residents under Article 4 (Residence), will be entitled to all benefits of the Convention.

Ownership/Base Erosion -- Subparagraph 1(c)

Subparagraph 1(c) provides a two part test, the so-called ownership and base erosion test. This test applies to any form of legal entity that is a resident of a Contracting State. Both prongs of the test must be satisfied for the resident to be entitled to benefits under subparagraph 1(c).

The ownership prong of the test, under clause i), requires that more than 50 percent of the beneficial interest in the person (in the case of a corporation, more than 50 percent of the number of shares of each class of its shares) be owned by persons who are themselves entitled to benefits under the other tests of paragraph 1 (*i.e.*, subparagraphs a), b), d), e) or f)) or who are citizens of the United States. The ownership may be indirect, although it is to be understood that the indirect ownership must be through persons that are themselves entitled to benefits under paragraph 1 or are U.S. citizens.

Trusts may be entitled to benefits under this provision if they are treated as residents under Article 4 (Residence) and they otherwise satisfy the requirements of this subparagraph. For purposes of this subparagraph, the beneficial interests in a trust will be considered to be owned by its beneficiaries in proportion to each beneficiary's actuarial interest in the trust. The interest of a remainder beneficiary will be equal to 100 percent less the aggregate percentages held by income beneficiaries. A beneficiary's interest in a trust will not be considered to be owned by a person entitled to benefits under the other provisions of paragraph 1 or who is a U.S. citizen if it is not possible to determine the beneficiary's actuarial interest. Consequently, if it is not possible to determine the actuarial interest of any beneficiaries in a trust, the ownership test under clause i) cannot be satisfied, unless all beneficiaries are persons entitled to benefits under the other subparagraphs of paragraph 1 or are U.S. citizens.

The base erosion prong of the test under subparagraph 1(c) requires that more than 50 percent of the person's gross income not be used, directly or indirectly, to meet liabilities, including liabilities for interest or royalties, to persons not entitled to the benefits under the other tests of paragraph 1 (i.e., subparagraphs a), b), d), e) or f)) or who not are citizens of the United States.

The term "gross income" is not defined in the Convention. Thus, in accordance with paragraph 2 of Article 3 (General Definitions), in determining whether a person deriving income from United States sources is entitled to the benefits of the Convention, the United States will ascribe the meaning to the term that it has in the United States. In such cases, "gross income" will be defined as gross receipts less cost of goods sold.

Publicly-Traded Corporations -- Subparagraph 1(d)

Subparagraphs (d) and (e) of paragraph 1 apply to two categories of corporations: publicly-traded corporations and subsidiaries of publicly-traded corporations. Clause (i) of subparagraph 1(d) provides that a company will be entitled to all the benefits of the Convention if there is substantial and regular trading in the company's principal class of shares on a "recognized stock exchange" located in either State. The term "recognized stock exchange" is defined in paragraph 5.

If a company has only one class of shares, it is only necessary to consider whether the shares of that class are regularly traded on a recognized stock exchange. If the company has more than one class of shares, it is necessary as an initial matter to determine the principal class of shares. The term "principal class of shares" is to be interpreted as the class of shares that represents the majority of the voting power and value of the company. When no single class of shares represents the majority of the voting power and value of the company, the "principal class of shares" is generally those classes that in the aggregate possess more than 50 percent of the voting power and value of the company. The term "shares" shall include depository receipts thereof or trust certificates thereof. In determining voting power, any shares or class of shares that are authorized but not issued shall not be counted; and, in mutual agreement between the competent authorities, appropriate weight shall be given to any restrictions or limitations on voting rights of, or entitlement to disproportionately higher participation in, issued shares.

The term "substantial and regular trading" is not defined in the Convention. In accordance with paragraph 2 of Article 3 (General Definitions), the term will be defined by reference to the domestic tax laws of the State from which treaty benefits are sought, generally the source State. In the case of the United States, this term is to be understood to have the meaning given "regularly traded" in Treas. Reg. section 1.884-5(d)(4)(i)(B), relating to the branch tax provisions of the Code. Under these regulations, a class of shares is considered to be "regularly traded" if two requirements are met: trades in the class of shares are made in more than de minimis quantities on at least 60 days during the taxable year, and the aggregate number of shares in the class traded during the year is at least 10 percent of the average number of shares outstanding during the year. Sections 1.884-5(d)(4)(i)(A), (ii) and (iii) will not be taken into account for purposes of defining the term "substantial and regular trading" under the Convention.

The substantial and regular trading requirement can be met by trading on any recognized exchange or exchanges located in either State. Trading on one or more recognized stock exchanges may be aggregated for purposes of this requirement. Thus, a U.S. company could satisfy the substantial and regular trading requirement through trading, in whole or in part, on a recognized stock exchange located in Thailand. Authorized but unissued shares are not considered for purposes of this test.

Subsidiaries of Publicly-Traded Corporations -- Subparagraph 1(e)

Subparagraph 1(e) provides a test under which certain companies that are directly or indirectly wholly owned by companies satisfying the publicly-traded test of subparagraph 1(d) may be entitled to the benefits of the Convention. Under this test, a company will be entitled to the benefits of the Convention if the company is wholly owned by a company described in subparagraph 1(d).

Subparagraph 1(e) permits indirect ownership. Consequently, the ownership by a publicly-traded company described in subparagraph (d) need not be direct. However, each intermediate owner in the chain of ownership must be a resident of a Contracting State.

Tax Exempt Organizations -- Subparagraph 1(f)

Subparagraph 1(f) provides that certain not-for-profit organizations will be entitled to all the benefits of the Convention. These entities are entities that by virtue of their not-for-profit status generally are exempt from tax in their Contracting State of residence, as long as more than half of the beneficiaries, members or participants, if any, in such organization are persons entitled under this Article to the benefits of the Convention. For purposes of this provision, the term "beneficiaries" should be understood to refer to the persons receiving benefits from the organization.

It is intended that all of the provisions of paragraph 1 will be self executing. Unlike the provisions of paragraph 4, discussed below, claiming benefits under paragraph 1 does not require advance competent authority ruling or approval. The tax authorities may, of course, on review, determine that the taxpayer has improperly interpreted the paragraph and is not entitled to the benefits claimed.

Paragraph 2

Paragraph 2 sets forth two tests under which a resident of a Contracting State that is not generally entitled to benefits of the Convention under paragraph 1 may receive treaty benefits with respect to certain items of income that are connected with or incidental to an active trade or business conducted in its State of residence.

Subparagraph 2(a) sets forth a two-pronged test that if satisfied entitles a resident of a Contracting State to the benefits of the Convention with respect to a particular item of income. First, the income must be derived from the other State and must be derived in connection with an active trade or business in which the resident engages in its State of residence. Second, the trade or business must be substantial in relation to the business or activity in the other State giving rise to the item of income.

Subparagraph 2(b) provides a second test. A resident of a Contracting State shall be entitled to the benefits of the Convention with respect to a particular item of income if the income is derived from the other Contracting State and is incidental to an active trade or business in which the resident engages in its State of residence.

The determinations required for each test are made separately for each item of income derived from the other State. It therefore is possible that a person would be entitled to the benefits of the Convention with respect to one item of income but not with respect to another. If a resident of a Contracting State is entitled to treaty benefits with respect to a particular item of income under paragraph 2, the resident is entitled to all benefits of the Convention insofar as they affect the taxation of that item of income in the other State. Set forth below is a more detailed discussion of the two disjunctive tests under paragraph 2.

Trade or Business -- Subparagraphs 2(a) and (b)

The term "trade or business" is not defined in the Convention. Pursuant to paragraph 2 of Article 3 (General Definitions), when determining whether a resident of the other State is entitled to the benefits of the Convention under paragraph 2 with respect to income derived from U.S.

sources, the United States will ascribe to this term the meaning that it has under the law of the United States. Accordingly, the United States competent authority will refer to the regulations issued under section 367(a) for the definition of the term "trade or business." In general, therefore, a trade or business will be considered to be a specific unified group of activities that constitute or could constitute an independent economic enterprise carried on for profit. Furthermore, a corporation generally will be considered to carry on a trade or business only if the officers and employees of the corporation conduct substantial managerial and operational activities. See, Code section 367(a)(3) and the regulations thereunder.

Notwithstanding this general definition of trade or business, paragraph 2 provides that the business of making or managing investments, when part of banking or insurance activities conducted by a bank or insurance company, will be considered to be a trade or business. Conversely, such activities conducted by a person other than a bank or insurance company will not be considered to be the conduct of an active trade or business, nor would they be considered to be the conduct of an active trade or business if conducted by a banking or insurance company but not as part of the company's banking or insurance business.

Because a headquarters operation is in the business of managing investments, a company that functions solely as a headquarter company will not be considered to be engaged in an active trade or business for purposes of paragraph 2.

Derived in Connection With Requirement of Subparagraph 2(a) Test -- Subparagraph 2(a)(i)

It is to be understood that income is derived in connection with a trade or business if the income-producing activity in the other State is a line of business that forms a part of or is complementary to the trade or business conducted in the State of residence by the income recipient. Although no definition of the terms "forms a part of" or "complementary" is set forth in the Convention, it is intended that a business activity generally will be considered to "form a part of" a business activity conducted in the other State if the two activities involve the design, manufacture or sale of the same products or type of products, or the provision of similar services. In order for two activities to be considered to be "complementary," the activities need not relate to the same types of products or services, but they should be part of the same overall industry and be related in the sense that the success or failure of one activity will tend to result in success or failure for the other. In cases in which more than one trade or business is conducted in the other State and only one of the trades or businesses forms a part of or is complementary to a trade or business conducted in the State of residence, it is necessary to identify the trade or business to which an item of income is attributable. Royalties generally will be considered to be derived in connection with the trade or business to which the underlying intangible property is attributable. Dividends will be deemed to be derived first out of earnings and profits of the treaty-benefitted trade or business, and then out of other earnings and profits. Interest income may be allocated under any reasonable method consistently applied. A method that conforms to U.S. principles for expense allocation will be considered a reasonable method. The following examples illustrate the application of this understanding.

Example 1. USCo is a corporation resident in the United States. USCo is engaged in an active manufacturing business in the United States. USCo owns 100 percent of the shares of ThaiCo, a corporation resident in Thailand. ThaiCo distributes USCo products in Thailand. Since the business activities conducted by the two corporations involve the same products, ThaiCo's distribution business is considered to form a part of USCo's manufacturing business for purposes of subparagraph 2(a)(i).

Example 2. The facts are the same as in Example 1, except that USCo does not manufacture. Rather, USCo operates a large research and development facility in the United States that licenses intellectual property to affiliates worldwide, including ThaiCo. ThaiCo and other USCo affiliates then manufacture and market the USCo-designed products in their respective markets. Since the activities conducted by ThaiCo and USCo involve the same product lines, these activities are considered to form a part of the same trade or business.

Example 3. Americair is a corporation resident in the United States that operates an international airline. ThaiSub is a wholly-owned subsidiary of Americair resident in Thailand. ThaiSub operates a chain of hotels in Thailand that are located near airports served by Americair flights. Americair frequently sells tour packages that include air travel to Thailand and lodging at ThaiSub hotels. Although both companies are engaged in the active conduct of a trade or business, the businesses of operating a chain of hotels and operating an airline are distinct trades or businesses. Therefore ThaiSub's business does not form a part of Americair's business. However, ThaiSub's business is considered to be complementary to Americair's business because they are part of the same overall industry (travel) and the links between their operations tend to make them interdependent.

Example 4. The facts are the same as in Example 3, except that ThaiSub owns an office building in Thailand instead of a hotel chain. No part of Americair's business is conducted through the office building. ThaiSub's business is not considered to form a part of or to be complementary to Americair's business. They are engaged in distinct trades or businesses in separate industries, and there is no economic dependence between the two operations.

Example 5. USFlower is a corporation resident in the United States. USFlower produces and sells flowers in the United States and other countries. USFlower owns all the shares of ThaiHolding, a corporation resident in Thailand. ThaiHolding is a holding company that is not engaged in a trade or business. ThaiHolding owns all the shares of three corporations that are resident in Thailand: ThaiFlower, ThaiLawn, and ThaiFish. ThaiFlower distributes USFlower flowers under the USFlower trademark in Thailand. ThaiLawn markets a line of lawn care products in Thailand under the USFlower trademark. In addition to being sold under the same trademark, ThaiLawn and ThaiFlower products are sold in the same stores and sales of each company's products tend to generate increased sales of the other's products. ThaiFish imports fish from the United States and distributes it to fish wholesalers in Thailand. For purposes of paragraph 2, the business of ThaiFlower forms a part of the business of USFlower, the business of

ThaiLawn is complementary to the business of USFlower, and the business of ThaiFish is neither part of nor complementary to that of USFlower.

Substantiality Requirement of Subparagraph 2(a) Test -- Subparagraph 2(a)(ii)

As indicated above, subparagraph 2(a)(ii) provides that income that a resident of a State derives from the other State will be entitled to the benefits of the Convention under paragraph 2(a) only if the income is derived in connection with a trade or business conducted in the recipient's State of residence and that trade or business is "substantial" in relation to the income-producing activity in the other State. It is to be understood that whether the trade or business of the income recipient is substantial will be determined based on all the facts and circumstances. These circumstances generally would include the relative scale of the activities conducted in the two States and the relative contributions made to the conduct of the trade or businesses in the two States.

Incidental Requirement of Subparagraph 2(b) Test -- Subparagraph 2(b)

A resident in one of the States also will be entitled to the benefits of the Convention with respect to an item of income if the income is derived from the other State and if the income is "incidental" to the trade or business conducted in the recipient's State of residence. The term "incidental" is not defined in the Convention, but it is to be understood that income derived from a State will be incidental to a trade or business conducted in the other State if the production of such income facilitates the conduct of the trade or business in the other State. An example of incidental income is the temporary investment of working capital derived from a trade or business.

Paragraph 3

Paragraph 3 provides that a Thai resident that is an "international banking facility" under the laws of Thailand or that is subject to the same taxation treatment under the laws of Thailand as an international banking facility shall not be entitles to any U.S. benefits under the Convention with respect to any income such resident receives from the United States.

Paragraph 4

Paragraph 4 provides that a person that is not entitled to the benefits of the Convention pursuant to paragraphs 1, 2 and 3 of this Article may be granted benefits under the Convention if the competent authority of the State in which the income in question arises so determines. This discretionary provision is included in recognition of the fact that, with the increasing scope and diversity of international economic relations, there may be cases where significant participation by third country residents in an enterprise of a Contracting State is warranted by sound business practice or long-standing business structures and does not necessarily indicate a motive of attempting to derive unintended Convention benefits.

The competent authority of a State will base a determination under this paragraph on whether the establishment, acquisition, or maintenance of the person seeking benefits under the Convention, or the conduct of such person's operations, has or had as one of its principal purposes the obtaining of benefits under the Convention. Thus, persons that establish operations in one of the States with the principal purpose of obtaining the benefits of the Convention ordinarily will not be granted relief under paragraph 4.

The competent authority may determine to grant all benefits of the Convention, or it may determine to grant only certain benefits. For instance, it may determine to grant benefits only with respect to a particular item of income in a manner similar to paragraph 2. Further, the competent authority may set time limits on the duration of any relief granted.

It is assumed that, for purposes of implementing paragraph 4, a taxpayer will not be required to wait until the tax authorities of one of the States have determined that benefits are denied before he will be permitted to seek a determination under this paragraph. In these circumstances, it is also expected that if the competent authority determines that benefits are to be allowed, they will be allowed retroactively to the time of entry into force of the relevant treaty provision or the establishment of the structure in question, whichever is later.

Paragraph 5

Paragraph 5 provides that the term "recognized stock exchange" means (i) the NASDAQ System owned by the National Association of Securities Dealers, and any stock exchange registered with the Securities and Exchange Commission as a national securities exchange for purposes of the Securities Exchange Act of 1934; (ii) any securities exchange recognized by the Securities and Exchange Commission of Thailand; and (ii) any stock exchange agreed upon by the competent authorities of the Contracting States.

Paragraph 6

Paragraph 6 provides that if income arising in one of the Contracting States is relieved in whole or in part from tax in that Contracting State under any provision of this Convention and a person is subject to tax in respect of the such income under the law in force in the other Contracting State by reference to the amount of the income which is remitted to or received in that other Contracting State (as opposed to being subject to tax by reference to the full amount of the income), then the relief to be allowed under the Convention in the Contracting State in which the income arises shall apply only to so much of the income as is remitted to or received in the other Contracting State during the calendar year such income accrues or the next succeeding year.

Paragraph 7 provides that the competent authorities of the Contracting States shall exchange such information as is necessary for carrying out the provisions of this Article.

Article 19 (Artistes and Sportsmen)

This Article deals with the taxation in a Contracting State of artistes (i.e., performing artists and entertainers) and sportsmen resident in the other Contracting State from the performance of their services as such. The Article applies both to the income of an entertainer or sportsman who performs services on his own behalf and one who performs services on behalf of another person, either as an employee of that person, or pursuant to any other arrangement. The rules of this Article take precedence over those of Articles 15 (Independent Personal Services) and 16 (Dependent Personal Services).

This Article applies only with respect to the income of performing artists and sportsmen. Others involved in a performance or athletic event, such as producers, directors, technicians, managers, coaches, etc., remain subject to the provisions of Articles 15 and 16. In addition, except as provided in paragraph 2, income earned by legal persons is not covered by Article 19.

Paragraph 1

Paragraph 1 describes the circumstances in which a Contracting State may tax the performance income of an entertainer or sportsman who is a resident of the other Contracting State. Under the paragraph, income derived by an individual resident of a Contracting State from activities as an entertainer or sportsman exercised in the other Contracting State may be taxed in that other State if the amount of the gross receipts derived by the performer exceeds the lesser of $100 (or its equivalent in the currency of Thailand) per day or $3,000 or its equivalent in Thai currency in the aggregate for the taxable year. This amount is the gross compensation for the services rendered. If the gross receipts exceed this amount, the full amount, not just the excess, may be taxed in the State of performance.

The OECD Model provides for taxation by the country of performance of the remuneration of entertainers or sportsmen with no dollar or time threshold. The Convention introduces the dollar threshold tests to distinguish between two groups of entertainers and athletes -- those who are paid large sums of money for very short periods of service, and who would, therefore, normally be exempt from host country tax under the standard personal services income rules, and those who earn relatively modest amounts and are, therefore, not easily distinguishable from those who earn other types of personal service income.

Tax may be imposed under paragraph 1 even if the performer would have been exempt from tax under Articles 15 (Independent Personal Services) or 16 (Dependent Personal Services).

On the other hand, if the performer would be exempt from host-country tax under Article 19, but would be taxable under either Article 15 or 16, tax may be imposed under either of those Articles. Thus, for example, if a performer derives remuneration from his activities in an independent capacity, and the remuneration is not attributable to a fixed base, he may be taxed by the host State in accordance with Article 19 if his remuneration exceeds the threshold amounts, despite the fact that he generally would be exempt from host State taxation under Article 15. However, a performer who receives less than the threshold amount and therefore is not taxable under Article 19, nevertheless may be subject to tax in the host country under Articles 15 or 16 if the tests for host-country taxability under those Articles are met. For example, if an entertainer who is an independent contractor earns $2,000 of income in a State for the calendar year, but the income is attributable to a fixed base regularly available to him in the State of performance, that State may tax his income under Article 15.

Since it frequently is not possible to know until year-end whether the income an entertainer or sportsman derived from a performance in a Contracting State will exceed the threshold amounts, nothing in the Convention precludes that Contracting State from withholding tax during the year and refunding after the close of the year if the taxability threshold has not been met.

As explained in paragraph 9 of the OECD Commentaries to Article 17 (Artistes and Sportsmen), Article 19 applies to all income connected with a performance by the entertainer, such as appearance fees, award or prize money, and a share of the gate receipts. Income derived from a Contracting State by a performer who is a resident of the other Contracting State from other than actual performance, such as royalties from record sales and payments for product endorsements, is not covered by this Article, but by other articles of the Convention, such as Article 12 (Royalties) or Article 15 (Independent Personal Services). For example, if an entertainer receives royalty income from the sale of live recordings, the royalty income would be subject to source country tax at a maximum rate of 5 percent under Article 12, even if the performance was conducted in the source country, although he could be taxed in the source country with respect to income from the performance itself under this Article if the dollar threshold is exceeded.

In determining whether income falls under Article 19 or another article, the controlling factor will be whether the income in question is predominantly attributable to the performance itself or other activities or property rights. For instance, a fee paid to a performer for endorsement of a performance in which the performer will participate would be considered to be so closely associated with the performance itself that it normally would fall within Article 19. Similarly, a sponsorship fee paid by a business in return for the right to attach its name to the performance would be so closely associated with the performance that it would fall under Article 19 as well. As indicated in paragraph 9 of the Commentaries to Article 17 of the OECD Model, a cancellation fee would not be considered to fall within Article 19 but would be dealt with under Article 7, 15 or 16.

As indicated in paragraph 4 of the Commentaries to Article 17 of the OECD Model, where an individual fulfills a dual role as performer and non-performer (such as a player-coach or an actor-director), but his role in one of the two capacities is negligible, the predominant character of the individual's activities should control the characterization of those activities. In other cases there should be an apportionment between the performance-related compensation and other compensation.

Consistently with Article 16 (Dependent Personal Services), Article 19 also applies regardless of the timing of actual payment for services. Thus, a bonus paid to a resident of a Contracting State with respect to a performance in the other Contracting State with respect to a particular taxable year would be subject to Article 19 for that year even if it was paid after the close of the year.

Paragraph 2

Paragraph 2 is intended to deal with the potential for abuse when a performer's income does not accrue directly to the performer himself, but to another person. Foreign performers commonly perform in the United States as employees of, or under contract with, a company or other person.

The relationship may truly be one of employee and employer, with no abuse of the tax system either intended or realized. On the other hand, the "employer" may, for example, be a company established and owned by the performer, which is merely acting as the nominal income recipient in respect of the remuneration for the performance (a "star company"). The performer may act as an "employee," receive a modest salary, and arrange to receive the remainder of the income from his performance in another form or at a later time. In such case, absent the provisions of paragraph 2, the star company arguably could escape host-country tax because it earns business profits but has no permanent establishment in that country. The performer may largely or entirely escape host-country tax by receiving only a small salary in the year the services are performed, perhaps small enough to place him below the dollar threshold in paragraph 1. The performer might arrange to receive further payments in a later year, when he is not subject to host-country tax, perhaps as deferred salary payments, dividends or liquidating distributions.

Paragraph 2 seeks to prevent this type of abuse while at the same time protecting the taxpayers' rights to the benefits of the Convention when there is a legitimate employee-employer relationship between the performer and the person providing his services. Under paragraph 2, when the income accrues to a person other than the performer, and the performer or related persons participate, directly or indirectly, in the receipts or profits of that other person, the income may be taxed in the Contracting State where the performer's services are exercised, without regard to the provisions of the Convention concerning business profits (Article 7), independent personal services (Article 15), or dependent personal services (Article 16). Thus, even if the "employer" has no permanent establishment or fixed base in the host country, its income may be subject to tax there under the provisions of paragraph 2. Taxation under paragraph 2 is on the person providing the services of the performer. This paragraph does not affect the rules of paragraph 1, which apply to the performer himself. The income taxable by virtue of paragraph 2 is reduced to the extent of salary payments to the performer, which fall under paragraph 1.

For purposes of paragraph 2, income is deemed to accrue to another person (i.e., the person providing the services of the performer) if that other person has control over, or the right to receive, gross income in respect of the services of the performer. Direct or indirect participation in the profits of a person may include, but is not limited to, the accrual or receipt of deferred remuneration, bonuses, fees, dividends, partnership income or other income or distributions.

Paragraph 2 does not apply if it is established that neither the performer nor any persons related to the performer participate directly or indirectly in the receipts or profits of the person providing the services of the performer. Assume, for example, that a circus owned by a U.S. corporation performs in Thailand, and promoters of the performance in Thailand pay the circus, which, in turn, pays salaries to the circus performers. The circus is determined to have no permanent establishment in Thailand. Since the circus performers do not participate in the profits of the circus, but merely receive their salaries out of the circus' gross receipts, the circus is protected by Article 7 and its income is not subject to host-country tax. Whether the salaries of the circus performers are subject to host-country tax under this Article depends on whether they exceed the thresholds in paragraph 1.

Since pursuant to Article 1 (General Scope) the Convention only applies to persons who are residents of one of the Contracting States, if the star company is not a resident of one of the Contracting States then taxation of the income is not affected by Article 19 or any other provision of the Convention.

This exception from paragraph 2 for non-abusive cases is not found in the OECD Model. The United States has entered a reservation to the OECD Model on this point.

Paragraph 3

Paragraph 3 provides an exception to the rules of paragraphs 1 and 2 in the case of a visit to a Contracting State by a public entertainer who is a resident of the other Contracting State, if the visit is substantially supported by public funds of his state of residence, including any political subdivision or local authority of that State. In the circumstances described, only the Contracting State of residence of the public entertainer may tax his income from performances. Although this rule is not found in the U.S. or OECD Models, a similar exception is provided in some other U.S. treaties.

Relation to Other Articles

This Article is subject to the provisions of the saving clause of paragraph 2 of Article 1 (Personal Scope). Thus, if an entertainer or a sportsman who is resident in Thailand is a citizen of the United States, the United States may tax all of his income from performances in the United States without regard to the provisions of this Article. In addition, benefits of this Article are subject to the provisions of Article 18 (Limitation on Benefits).

Article 20 (Pensions and Social Security Payments)

Article 20 deals with the taxation of private (i.e., non-government) pensions, annuities, social security, and similar benefits.

Paragraph 1

Paragraph 1 provides that private pensions and other similar remuneration paid in consideration of past employment are generally taxable only in the residence State of the recipient. It is understood that the rules of this paragraph apply even if the payee of the pension is not the person who performed the past employment. For example, a pension paid to a surviving spouse who is a resident of Thailand would be exempt from tax by the United States on the same basis as if the right to the pension had been earned directly by the surviving spouse. A pension may be paid periodically or in a lump sum. The rules of this paragraph do not apply to government service pensions, which are dealt with in paragraph 2 of Article 21 (Government Service), nor do they deal with social security benefits, which are dealt with in paragraph 2 of Article 20.

The phrase "pensions and other similar remuneration" is intended to encompass payments made by private retirement plans and arrangements in consideration of past employment. In the United States, the plans encompassed by Paragraph 1 include: qualified plans under section 401(a), individual retirement plans (including individual retirement plans that are part of a simplified employee pension plan that satisfies section 408(k), individual retirement accounts and section 408(p) accounts), non-discriminatory section 457 plans, section 403(a) qualified annuity plans, and section 403(b) plans. The Competent Authorities may agree that distributions from other plans that generally meet similar criteria to those applicable to other plans established under their respective laws also qualify for the benefits of Paragraph 1. In the United States, these criteria are as follows:

a) The plan must be written;

b) In the case of an employer-maintained plan, the plan must be nondiscriminatory insofar as it (alone or in combination with other comparable plans) must cover a wide range of employees. including rank and file employees, and actually provide significant benefits for the entire range of covered employees;

c) In the case of an employer-maintained plan the plan must contain provisions that severely limit the employees' ability to use plan assets for purposes other than retirement, and in all cases be subject to tax provisions that discourage participants from using the assets for purposes other than retirement; and

d) The plan must provide for payment of a reasonable level of benefits at death, a stated age, or an event related to work status, and otherwise require minimum distributions under rules designed to ensure that any death benefits provided to the participants' survivors are merely incidental to the retirement benefits provided to the participants.

In addition, certain distribution requirements must be met before distributions from these plans would fall under paragraph 1. To qualify as a pension distribution or similar remuneration from a U.S. plan the employee must have been either employed by the same employer for five years or be at least 62 years old at the time of the distribution. In addition, the distribution must be made either (A) on account of death or disability, (B) as part of a series of substantially equal payments over the employee's life expectancy (or over the joint life expectancy of the employee and a beneficiary), or (c) after the employee attained the age of 55. Finally, the distribution must be made either after separation from service or on or after attainment of age 65. A distribution from a pension plan solely due to termination of the pension plan is not a distribution falling under paragraph 1.

Paragraph 2

The treatment of social security benefits is dealt with in paragraph 2. This paragraph provides that, notwithstanding the provision of paragraph 1 under which private pensions are taxable exclusively in the State of residence of the beneficial owner, payments made by one of the Contracting States as a social security benefit or similar public pension to a resident of the other Contracting State or to a citizen of the United States will be taxable only in the Contracting State making the payment. This paragraph applies to social security beneficiaries whether they have contributed to the system as private sector or government employees.

The phrase "similar public pension" is intended to include United States tier 1 Railroad Retirement benefits. The reference to U.S. citizens is necessary to insure that a social security payment by Thailand to a U.S. citizen not resident in the United States will not be taxed by the United States.

Paragraph 3

Under paragraph 3, annuities that are derived and beneficially owned by a resident of a Contracting State are taxable only in that State. An annuity, as the term is used in this paragraph, means a stated sum paid periodically at stated times during a specified number of years, under an obligation to make the payment in return for adequate and full consideration (other than for services rendered). An annuity received in consideration for services rendered would be treated as deferred compensation and generally taxable in accordance with Article 16 (Dependent Personal Services).

Paragraphs 4 and 5

Paragraphs 4 and 5 deal with alimony and child support payments. Both alimony, under paragraph 4, and child support payments, under paragraph 5, are defined as periodic payments made pursuant to a written separation agreement or a decree of divorce, separate maintenance, or compulsory support. Paragraph 4, however, deals only with payments of that type that are taxable to the payee. Under that paragraph, alimony paid by a resident of a Contracting State to a resident of the other Contracting State is taxable under the Convention only in the State of residence of the recipient. Paragraph 5 deals with those periodic payments that are for the support of a child and that are not covered by paragraph 4 (i.e., those payments that are not taxable to the payee). These types of payments by a resident of a Contracting State to a resident of the other Contracting State are taxable only in the first-mentioned Contracting State.

Relation to Other Articles

Paragraphs 1, 3 and 4 of Article 20 are subject to the saving clause of paragraph 2 of Article 1 (Personal Scope). Thus, a U.S. citizen who is resident in the other Contracting State, and receives either a pension, annuity or alimony payment from the United States, may be subject to U.S. tax on the payment, notwithstanding the rules in those three paragraphs that give the State of residence of the recipient the exclusive taxing right. Paragraphs 2 and 5 are excepted from the saving clause by virtue of paragraph 3(a) of Article 1. Thus, the United States will allow U.S. citizens and residents the benefits of paragraph 5.

Article 21 (Government Service)

Article 21 deals with the taxation of income (including pensions) from governmental employment. It generally follows the corresponding provisions of both the U.S. and OECD Models.

Paragraph 1

Subparagraphs a) and b) of paragraph 1 deal with the taxation of government compensation other than a pension. Subparagraph a) provides the general rule that wages, salaries, and other remuneration paid by one of the Contracting States or by its political subdivisions or local authorities to any individual are generally exempt from tax by the other State, if the compensation is in respect of governmental services rendered to that State, subdivision or authority. Under subparagraph b), however, such payments are taxable only in the other State if the services are rendered there and if the individual is a resident of that State who is either a national (i.e., in the case of the United States, a citizen) of that State or who did not become resident of that State solely for purposes of rendering the services. Thus, an individual who, after establishing U.S. residence, is hired by the Thai Embassy in Washington, would be subject to U.S. (and not Thai) tax on his Thai salary. The paragraph applies both to governmental employees and to independent contractors engaged by governments to perform governmental services for them.

Paragraph 2

Paragraph 2 deals with the taxation of a pension paid by, or out of funds created by, one of the States or a political subdivision or a local authority thereof to an individual in respect of services rendered to that State or subdivision or authority. Subparagraph a) provides the general rule that such a pension is taxable only by the paying State. Subparagraph b), however, provides an exception under which such a pension is taxable only in the residence State if the individual is a resident of, and a national of, that other State. Pensions paid to retired civilian and military employees of a Government of either State are intended to be covered under paragraph 2. When benefits paid by a State in respect of services rendered to that State or a subdivision or authority are in the form of social security benefits, however, those payments are covered by paragraph 2 of Article 20 (Pensions and Social Security Payments). As a general matter, the result will be the same whether Article 20 or 21 applies, since social security benefits are taxable exclusively by the source country and so are government pensions. The result will differ only when the payment is made to a citizen and resident of the other Contracting State, who is not also a citizen of the paying State. In such a case, social security benefits continue to be taxable at source while government pensions become taxable only in the residence country.

Paragraph 3

Paragraph 3 provides that the provisions of Articles 16 (Dependent Personal Services), 17 (Directors' Fees), and 20 (Pensions and Social Security Payments) shall apply to remuneration and pensions in respect of services rendered in connection with a business carried on by one of the States or a political subdivision or a local authority thereof.

Relation to Other Articles

Under paragraph 3(b) of Article 1 (Personal Scope), the saving clause (paragraph 2 of Article 1) does not apply to the benefits conferred by one of the States under this Article if the recipient of the benefits is neither a citizen of, nor has immigrant status in, that State. Thus, for example, a Thai resident who receives a pension paid by Thailand in respect of services rendered to the Government of Thailand shall be taxable on this pension only in Thailand unless the individual is a U.S. citizen or acquires a U.S. green card.

Article 22 (Students and Trainees)

This Article differs from the U.S. Model in order to reflect the particular economic and cultural relationships in this area between the United States and Thailand. This Article reflects the important benefits to each country from the student and trainee exchanges the Article covers.

Paragraph 1

Paragraph 1 of this Article generally provides that a resident of a Contracting State who visits the other Contracting State for the primary purpose of studying at a university or other recognized educational institution, securing training in a professional specialty, or studying or doing research as the recipient of a grant from a government or a charitable institution shall be exempt from tax in that Contracting State with respect to certain items of income during that period of study, research or training provided certain conditions are met. Paragraph 1(b) defines those exempt items of income as: (1) payments from abroad for maintenance, education, study, research, or training; (2) grants, allowances or awards; and (3) income from personal services performed in that other Contracting State to the extent of $3,000 United States dollars or its equivalent in Thai currency per taxable year. The exemptions provided in paragraph 1 are available to the visiting student or trainee for a period not exceeding five taxable years from the beginning of the visit.

The reference in paragraph 1 to "primary purpose" is meant to describe individuals participating in a full time program of study, training or research, the term used in the U.S. Model. "Primary purpose" was substituted for the reference in the OECD Model to "exclusive purpose" to prevent too narrow an interpretation. It is not the intention to exclude full time students who, in accordance with their visas, may hold part time employment jobs.

A student must be studying at a recognized educational institution. An educational institution is understood to be an institution that normally maintains a regular faculty and normally has a regular body of students in attendance at the place where the educational activities are carried on. An educational institution will be considered to be recognized if it is accredited by an authority that generally is responsible for accreditation of institutions in the particular field of study.

The host-country exemption in the Article applies in subparagraph (b)(i) to gifts received by the student from abroad for the purpose of his maintenance, education or training. A payment will be considered to be from abroad if the payor is located outside the host State. In all cases substance over form should prevail in determining the identity of the payor. Consequently, payments made directly or indirectly by the U.S. person with whom the visitor is training, but which have been routed through a non-host-country source, such as, for example, a foreign bank account, should not be treated as arising outside the United States for this purpose.

Paragraph 2

Paragraph 2 of this Article generally provides an exemption for residents of a Contracting State who are employed by, or under contract with, a resident of the same Contracting State and who temporarily visit the other Contracting State for the purpose of studying at a university or other recognized educational institution, or acquiring technical, professional, or business experience in that other Contracting State, provided such training is from a person other than the employer or contractor. Such student or trainee is exempt from taxation in the other Contracting State for a period not in excess of twelve consecutive months on personal services income to the extent of $7,500 (or the equivalent in Thai currency) during that period. In addition, the student or trainee is exempt from taxation in the other Contracting State on expenses reimbursed to him or borne on his behalf.

Paragraph 3

Paragraph 3 of this Article deals with a resident of a Contracting State who is temporarily present in the other Contracting State for a period not exceeding one year, as a participant in a program sponsored by the Government of the host State, for the primary purpose of training, research or study. Such an individual will be exempt from tax by the host State on compensation for personal services in respect of such training, research or study performed in the host State in an aggregate amount not exceeding $10,000 United States dollars (or its equivalent in Thai currency) during a taxable year. In addition, the participant is exempt from taxation in the other Contracting State on expenses reimbursed to him or borne on his behalf.

Paragraph 4

Paragraph 4 of this Article provides that the benefits provided under Article 23 (Teachers) and the benefits of paragraph 1 of this Article, when taken together, shall extend for such period of time, not to exceed five years from the date of arrival of the person claiming such benefits, as may be reasonable or customarily required to effectuate the purpose of the visit. The benefits of Article 23 (Teachers) are not available to an individual who during the immediately preceding period enjoyed the benefits of paragraph 1 of this Article.

The exemptions in this Article apply in addition to, and not in lieu of, any allowance (e.g., personal exemptions and deductions) available to the person under the internal laws of the Contracting States. If the amount earned exceeds the specified amount per annum, only the excess is subject to tax.

Relation to Other Articles

Under paragraph 3(b) of Article 1 (Personal Scope), the saving clause (paragraph 2 of Article 1) does not apply to this Article if the individual is neither a citizen of the host State nor has been admitted for permanent residence there. The saving clause, however, does apply with respect to citizens and permanent residents of the host State. Thus, a U.S. citizen who is a resident of Thailand and who visits the United States as a full-time student at an accredited university will not be exempt from U.S. tax on remittances from abroad that otherwise constitute U.S. taxable income. A person, however, who is not a U.S. citizen, and who visits the United States as a student and remains long enough to become a resident under U.S. law, but does not become a permanent resident (i.e., does not acquire a green card), will be entitled to the full benefits of the Article.

Article 23 (Teachers)

Paragraph 1

Paragraph 1 provides an exemption from tax in one Contracting State for an individual who visits that State (the "host State") for a period not exceeding two years for the purpose of teaching or engaging in research at a university, college or other recognized educational institution in that State. This rule applies only if the individual is a resident of the other Contracting State immediately before his visit begins. The exemption applies to any remuneration for such teaching or research. The exemption from tax applies only if the visit does not exceed two years from the date he first visits the host State for the purpose of teaching or engaging in research at a university, college or other recognized educational institution there.

The host State exemption will apply if the teaching or research is carried on at an accredited university, college, school or other recognized educational institution. An educational institution will be considered to be accredited if it is accredited by an authority that generally is responsible for accreditation of institutions in the particular field of study.

Paragraph 2

Paragraph 2 provides that the Article shall apply to income from research only if such research is undertaken by the individual in the public interest and not primarily for the benefit of some other private person or persons.

Relation to Other Articles

Under paragraph 3(b) of Article 1 (Personal Scope), the saving clause (paragraph 2 of Article 1) does not apply to the benefits conferred by one of the States under this Article if the recipient of the benefits is neither a citizen of that State, nor, in the case of the United States, a lawful permanent resident (i.e., a "green card" holder). Thus, a resident of Thailand who visits the United States for two academic years as a professor and becomes a U.S. resident according to the Code, other than by virtue of acquiring a green card, would continue to be exempt from U.S. tax in accordance with this article so long as he is not a U.S. citizen and does not acquire immigrant status in the United States. The saving clause does apply in this case to U.S. citizens and immigrants.

Article 24 (Other Income)

Article 24 generally assigns taxing jurisdiction over income not dealt with in the other articles (Articles 6 through 23) of the Convention to the State of residence of the beneficial owner of the income and defines the terms necessary to apply the article. However, the other State may also tax such income if it arises in the other State. An item of income is "dealt with" in another article if it is the type of income described in the article and it has its source in a Contracting State. For example, all royalty income that arises in a Contracting State and that is beneficially owned by a resident of the other Contracting State is "dealt with" in Article 12 (Royalties).

Examples of items of income covered by Article 24 include income from gambling, punitive (but not compensatory) damages, covenants not to compete, and income from certain financial instruments to the extent derived by persons not engaged in the trade or business of dealing in such instruments (unless the transaction giving rise to the income is related to a trade or business, in which case it is dealt with under Article 7 (Business Profits)). The article also applies to items of income that are not dealt with in the other articles because of their source or some other characteristic. For example, Article 11 (Interest) addresses only the taxation of interest arising in a Contracting State. Interest arising in a third State that is not attributable to a permanent establishment, therefore, is subject to Article 24.

Distributions from partnerships and distributions from trusts are not generally dealt with under Article 24 because partnership and trust distributions generally do not constitute income. Under the Code, partners include in income their distributive share of partnership income annually, and partnership distributions themselves generally do not give rise to income. Also, under the Code, trust income and distributions have the character of the associated distributable net income and therefore would generally be covered by another article of the Convention. See Code section 641 et seq.

Paragraph 1

Paragraph 1 provides that items of income not dealt with in other articles that are earned by a resident of a Contracting State generally will be taxable in the State of residence. This right of taxation applies whether or not the residence State exercises its right to tax the income covered by the Article.

The residence taxation provided by paragraph 1 applies only when a resident of a Contracting State is the beneficial owner of the income. This is understood from the phrase "income of a resident of a Contracting State." Thus, source taxation of income not dealt with in other articles of the Convention is not limited by paragraph 1 if it is nominally paid to a resident of the other Contracting State, but is beneficially owned by a resident of a third State.

Paragraph 2

Paragraph 2 provides an exception to the general rule of paragraph 1 for income, other than income from real property, that is attributable to a permanent establishment or fixed base maintained in a Contracting State by a resident of the other Contracting State. The taxation of such income is governed by the provisions of Articles 7 (Business Profits) and 15 (Independent Personal Services). Therefore, income arising outside the United States that is attributable to a permanent establishment maintained in the United States by a resident of Thailand generally would be taxable by the United States under the provisions of Article 7. This would be true even if the income is sourced in a third State.

There is an exception to this general rule with respect to income a resident of a Contracting State derives from immovable (or real) property located outside the other Contracting State (whether in the first-mentioned Contracting State or in a third State) that is attributable to the resident's permanent establishment or fixed base in the other Contracting State. In such a case, only the first-mentioned Contracting State (i.e., the State of residence of the person deriving the income) and not the host State of the permanent establishment or fixed base may tax that income. This special rule for foreign-situs property is consistent with the general rule, also reflected in Article 6 (Income from Immovable (Real) Property), that only the situs and residence States may tax real property and real property income. Even if such property is part of the property of a permanent establishment or fixed base in a Contracting State, that State may not tax if neither the situs of the property nor the residence of the owner is in that State.

Paragraph 3

Paragraph 3 is not found in the U.S. or OECD Models. It is taken from the U.N. Model. It modifies the general rule of paragraph 1. It provides that, notwithstanding paragraphs 1 and 2, items of income of a resident of a Contracting State not dealt with in the other articles of the Convention and arising in the other Contracting State, may also be taxed in that other Contracting State. Thus, gambling income of a resident of the United States that arises in Thailand may be taxed both in the United States and in Thailand. Paragraph 1, therefore, provides exclusive residence-based taxation only to income of a resident of a Contracting State that does not arise in the other Contracting State.

Relation to Other Articles

This Article is subject to the saving clause of paragraph 2 of Article 1 (Personal Scope). Thus, the United States may tax the income of a resident of Thailand that is not dealt with elsewhere in the Convention, if that resident is a citizen of the United States. The Article is also subject to the provisions of Article 18 (Limitation on Benefits). Thus, if a resident of Thailand earns income that falls within the scope of paragraph 1 of Article 24, but that is taxable by the United States under U.S. law, the income would be exempt from U.S. tax under the provisions of Article 24 only if the resident satisfies one of the tests of Article 18 for entitlement to benefits.

Article 25 (Relief from Double Taxation)

This Article describes the manner in which each Contracting State undertakes to relieve double taxation. Both the United States and Thailand use the foreign tax credit method under their internal laws, and by treaty.

Paragraph 1

The United States agrees, in paragraph 1, to allow to its citizens and residents a credit against U.S. tax for income taxes paid or accrued to Thailand. Paragraph 1 also provides that Thailand's covered taxes are income taxes for U.S. purposes. This provision is based on the Treasury Department's review of Thailand's laws. The Treasury Department has determined that the Thai Petroleum Income Tax Act is a "tax in lieu of an income tax" under section 903 of the Internal Revenue Code.

The credit under the Convention is allowed in accordance with the provisions and subject to the conditions and limitations of U.S. law, as that law may be amended over time, so long as the general principle of this Article, i.e., the allowance of a credit, is retained. Thus, although the Convention provides for a foreign tax credit, the terms of the credit are determined by the provisions, at the time a credit is given, of the U.S. statutory credit.

Subparagraph (b) provides for a deemed-paid credit, consistent with section 902 of the Code, to a U.S. corporation in respect of dividends received from a corporation resident in Thailand of which the U.S. corporation owns at least 10 percent of the voting stock. This credit is for the tax paid by the Thai corporation on the profits out of which the dividends are considered paid.

As indicated, the U.S. credit under the Convention is subject to the various limitations of U.S. law (see Code sections 901 - 908). For example, the credit against U.S. tax generally is limited to the amount of U.S. tax due with respect to net foreign source income within the relevant foreign tax credit limitation category (see Code section 904(a) and (d)), and the dollar amount of the credit is determined in accordance with U.S. currency translation rules (see, e.g., Code section 986). Similarly, U.S. law applies to determine carryover periods for excess credits and other inter-year adjustments. When the alternative minimum tax is due, the alternative minimum tax foreign tax credit generally is limited in accordance with U.S. law to 90 percent of alternative minimum tax liability. Furthermore, nothing in the Convention prevents the limitation of the U.S. credit from being applied on a per-country basis (should internal law be changed), an overall basis, or to particular categories of income (see, e.g., Code section 865(h)).

The reference in paragraph 1 to the "conditions" of U.S. law is explained in an exchange of diplomatic notes, described below.

Paragraph 2

Paragraph 2 provides the specific rules under which Thailand, in imposing tax on its residents, provides relief for U.S. taxes paid by those residents. The paragraph requires that Thailand allow as a credit against Thai tax payable in respect of income any United States tax payable in respect of the income that is from sources within the United States. The credit under this paragraph is allowed in accordance with the provisions and subject to the limitations of Thai law, as that law may be amended over time, so long as the general principles of this Article (i.e., the allowance of a credit) is retained. The paragraph also provides that the credit shall not exceed that the Thai tax, determined without regard to the credit given, appropriate to the item of income. The paragraph shall not apply with respect to income that has been denied benefits of the Convention under the provisions of Article 18 (Limitation on Benefits).

Paragraph 3

Paragraph 3 provides the exclusive sourcing rules for purposes of allowing relief from double taxation pursuant this Article. Subparagraph 3(a) states that income derived by a resident of a Contracting State which under the Convention may be taxed in the other Contracting State (other than solely by reason of citizenship under the saving clause of paragraph 2 of Article 1(Personal Scope)) shall be deemed to arise in that other State. Subparagraph 3(b) states that income derived by a resident of a Contracting State which in accordance with this Convention may not be taxed in the other Contracting State shall be deemed to arise in that resident's Contracting State of residence.

The paragraph also provides, however, that, notwithstanding the general rules of subparagraphs (a) and (b), the determination of the source of income for purposes of double tax relief pursuant to this Article shall be subject to any source rules in the domestic laws of the Contracting State that apply to limit the foreign tax credit. In general, the source rules provided in the Convention are consistent with the Code source rules for foreign tax credit and other purposes. Where, however, the Convention and Code source rules are inconsistent, the Code source rules (e.g., Code section 904(g)) will be used to determine the limits for the allowance of a credit under the Convention. The paragraph also provides that the general source rules paragraph 3 shall not apply in determining foreign tax credits for taxes other than the taxes referred to in Article 2 (Taxes Covered).

Relation to Other Articles

By virtue of the exceptions in subparagraph 2(a) of Article 1 this Article is not subject to the saving clause of paragraph 2 of Article 1 (General Scope). Thus, the United States will allow a credit to its citizens and residents in accordance with the Article, even if such credit were to provide a benefit not available under the Code.

Exchange of Notes

Paragraph 1 of Article 25 of the treaty provides that the United States shall allow a credit for taxes paid to Thailand "subject to the *conditions and* limitations of the law of the United States..." (emphasis added). As stated in the diplomatic notes exchanged at the time of signature of the Convention, it was mutually understood that the addition of the word "conditions" is intended to make clear that U.S. rules regarding "dual capacity" taxpayers apply. The diplomatic notes also provide that if the United States alters its policy to authorize tax-sparing credits or grants such a credit in a tax treaty with another country, negotiations will be opened with a view to concluding a protocol that would amend the Convention to incorporate such a credit.

Article 26 (Non-discrimination)

This Article assures that nationals of a Contracting State, in the case of paragraph 1, and residents of a Contracting State, in the case of paragraphs 2 through 4, will not be subject, directly or indirectly, to discriminatory taxation in the other Contracting State. For this purpose, nondiscrimination means providing national treatment. Not all differences in tax treatment, either as between nationals of the two States, or between residents of the two States, are violations of this national treatment standard. Rather, the national treatment obligation of this Article applies only if the nationals or residents of the two States are comparably situated.

Each of the relevant paragraphs of the Article provides that two persons that are comparably situated must be treated similarly. Although the actual words differ from paragraph to paragraph (e.g., paragraph 1 refers to two nationals "in the same circumstances," paragraph 2 refers to two enterprises "carrying on the same activities" and paragraph 4 refers to two enterprises that are "similar"), the common underlying premise is that if the difference in treatment is directly related to a tax-relevant difference in the situations of the domestic and foreign persons being compared, that difference is not to be treated as discriminatory (e.g., if one person is taxable in a Contracting State on worldwide income and the other is not, or tax may be collectible from one person at a later stage, but not from the other, distinctions in treatment would be justified under paragraph 1). Other examples of such factors that can lead to non-discriminatory differences in treatment will be noted in the discussions of each paragraph.

The operative paragraphs of the Article also use different language to identify the kinds of differences in taxation treatment that will be considered discriminatory. For example, paragraphs 1 and 4 speak of "any taxation or any requirement connected therewith which is other or more burdensome," while paragraph 2 specifies that a tax "shall not be less favorably levied." Regardless of these differences in language, only differences in tax treatment that materially disadvantage the foreign person relative to the domestic person are properly the subject of the Article.

Paragraph 1

Paragraph 1 provides that a national of one Contracting State may not be subject to taxation or connected requirements in the other Contracting State that are other or more burdensome than the taxes and connected requirements imposed upon a national of that other State in the same circumstances. As noted above, whether or not the two persons are both taxable on worldwide income is a significant circumstance for this purpose. The term "other" does not simply refer to different requirements; the only relevant question under this provision should be whether the requirement imposed on a national of the other State is more burdensome. A requirement may be different from the requirements imposed on U.S. nationals without being more burdensome.

Thus, a national of a Contracting State is afforded protection under this paragraph even if the national is not a resident of either Contracting State. Accordingly, a U.S. citizen who is resident in a third country is entitled, under this paragraph, to the same treatment in Thailand as a national of Thailand who is in similar circumstances (i.e., presumably one who is resident in a third State). The term "national" in relation to a Contracting State is defined in subparagraph 1(j) of Article 3 (General Definitions).

Because the relevant circumstances referred to in the paragraph relate, among other things, to taxation on worldwide income, paragraph 1 does not obligate the United States to apply the same taxing regime to a national of Thailand who is not resident in the United States and a U.S. national who is not resident in the United States. United States citizens who are not residents of the United States but who are, nevertheless, subject to United States tax on their worldwide income are not in the same circumstances with respect to United States taxation as citizens of Thailand who are not United States residents. Thus, for example, Article 26 would not entitle a national of Thailand resident in a third country to taxation at graduated rates of U.S. source dividends or other investment income that applies to a U.S. citizen resident in the same third country.

In order to conform to the OECD Model, the definition of "national" in the Convention, as in the U.S. Model, extends beyond citizens to cover juridical persons that are nationals of a Contracting State as well. This expanded definition, however, generally may add little as a practical matter to the scope of the Article. A corporation that is a national of Thailand and is doing business in the United States is already protected, vis-a-vis a U.S. corporation, by paragraph 2. If a Thai corporation is not doing business in the United States it is, in relevant respect, in different circumstances from a U.S. corporation, and is, therefore, not entitled to national treatment in the United States. With respect to U.S. nationals claiming nondiscrimination protection from Thailand, U.S. juridical persons that are "nationals" of the United States are also

U.S. residents (e.g., U.S. corporations but not partnerships), and are, therefore, protected by paragraphs 2 and 4 in any event.

Paragraph 2

Paragraph 2 of the Article, like the comparable paragraph in the OECD Model, provides that a Contracting State may not tax a permanent establishment of an enterprise of the other Contracting State less favorably than an enterprise of that first-mentioned State that is carrying on the same activities. This provision, however, does not obligate a Contracting State to grant to an enterprise of the other Contracting State any tax allowances, reliefs, etc., that it grants to its own residents on account of their civil status or family responsibilities. Thus, if a sole proprietor who is a resident of Thailand has a permanent establishment in the United States, in assessing income tax on the profits attributable to the permanent establishment, the United States is not obligated to allow to the resident of Thailand the personal allowances for himself and his family that he would be permitted to take if the permanent establishment were a sole proprietorship owned and operated by a U.S. resident, despite the fact that the individual income tax rates would apply.

The fact that a U.S. permanent establishment of an enterprise of Thailand is subject to U.S. tax only on income that is attributable to the permanent establishment, while a U.S. corporation engaged in the same activities is taxable on its worldwide income is not, in itself, a sufficient difference to deny national treatment to the permanent establishment. There are cases, however, where the two enterprises would not be similarly situated and differences in treatment may be warranted. For instance, it would not be a violation of the nondiscrimination protection of paragraph 2 to require the Thai enterprise to provide information in a reasonable manner that may be different from the information requirements imposed on a resident enterprise, because information may not be as readily available to the Internal Revenue Service from a foreign as from a domestic enterprise. Similarly, it would not be a violation of paragraph 2 to impose penalties on persons who fail to comply with such a requirement (see, e.g., sections 874(a) and 882(c)(2)). Further, a determination that income and expenses have been attributed or allocated to a permanent establishment in conformity with the principles of Article 7 (Business Profits) implies that the attribution or allocation was not discriminatory.

Section 1446 of the Code imposes on any partnership with income that is effectively connected with a U.S. trade or business the obligation to withhold tax on amounts allocable to a foreign partner. In the context of the Convention, this obligation applies with respect to a share of the partnership income of a partner resident in Thailand, and attributable to a U.S. permanent establishment. There is no similar obligation with respect to the distributive shares of U.S. resident partners. It is understood, however, that this distinction is not a form of discrimination within the meaning of paragraph 2 of the Article. No distinction is made between U.S. and non-U.S. partnerships, since the law requires that partnerships of both U.S. and non-U.S. domicile withhold tax in respect of the partnership shares of non-U.S. partners. Furthermore, in distinguishing between U.S. and non-U.S. partners, the requirement to withhold on the non-U.S. but not the U.S. partner's share is not discriminatory taxation, but, like other withholding on nonresident aliens, is merely a reasonable method for the collection of tax from persons who are not continually present in the United States, and as to whom it otherwise may be difficult for the United States to enforce its tax jurisdiction. If tax has been over-withheld, the partner can, as in other cases of over-withholding, file for a refund. (The relationship between paragraph 2 and the imposition of the branch tax is dealt with below in the discussion of paragraph 5.)

Paragraph 3

Paragraph 3 prohibits discrimination in the allowance of deductions. When an enterprise of a Contracting State pays interest, royalties or other disbursements to a resident of the other Contracting State, the first-mentioned Contracting State must allow a deduction for those payments in computing the taxable profits of the enterprise as if the payment had been made under the same conditions to a resident of the first-mentioned Contracting State. An exception to this rule is provided for cases where the provisions of paragraph 1 of Article 9 (Associated Enterprises), paragraph 7 of Article 11 (Interest) or paragraph 6 of Article 12 (Royalties) apply, because all of these provisions permit the denial of deductions in certain circumstances in respect of transactions between related persons. This exception would include the denial or deferral of certain interest deductions under Code section 163(j).

The term "other disbursements" is understood to include a reasonable allocation of executive and general administrative expenses, research and development expenses and other expenses incurred for the benefit of a group of related persons that includes the person incurring the expense.

Paragraph 4

Paragraph 4 requires that a Contracting State not impose more burdensome taxation or connected requirements on an enterprise of that State that is wholly or partly owned or controlled, directly or indirectly, by one or more residents of the other Contracting State, than the taxation or connected requirements that it imposes on other similar enterprises of that first-mentioned Contracting State. For this purpose it is understood that "similar" refers to similar activities or ownership of the enterprise.

The Tax Reform Act of 1986 changed the rules for taxing corporations on certain distributions they make in liquidation. Prior to 1986, corporations were not taxed on distributions of appreciated property in complete liquidation, although nonliquidating distributions of the same property, with several exceptions, resulted in corporate-level tax. In part to eliminate this disparity, the law now generally taxes corporations on the liquidating distribution of appreciated property. The Code provides an exception in the case of distributions by 80 percent or more controlled subsidiaries to their parent corporations, on the theory that the built-in gain in the asset will be recognized when the parent sells or distributes the asset. This exception does not apply to distributions to parent corporations that are tax-exempt organizations or, except to the extent provided in regulations, foreign corporations. The policy of the legislation is to collect one corporate-level tax on the liquidating distribution of appreciated property. If, and only if, that tax can be collected on a subsequent sale or distribution does the legislation defer the tax. It is understood that the inapplicability of the exception to the tax on distributions to foreign parent corporations under section 367(e)(2) does not conflict with paragraph 4 of the Article. While a liquidating distribution to a U.S. parent will not be taxed, and, except to the extent provided in regulations, a liquidating distribution to a foreign parent will, paragraph 4 merely prohibits discrimination among corporate taxpayers on the basis of U.S. or foreign stock ownership. Eligibility for the exception to the tax on liquidating distributions for distributions to non-exempt, U.S. corporate parents is not based upon the nationality of the owners of the distributing corporation, but rather is based upon whether such owners would be subject to corporate tax if they subsequently sold or distributed the same property. Thus, the exception does not apply to distributions to persons that would not be so subject -- not only foreign corporations, but also tax-exempt organizations. A similar analysis applies to the treatment of section 355 distributions subject to section 367(e)(1).

For the reasons given above in connection with the discussion of paragraph 2 of the Article, it is also understood that the provision in section 1446 of the Code for withholding of tax on Thai partners does not violate paragraph 4 of the Article.

It is further understood that the ineligibility of a U.S. corporation with nonresident alien shareholders to make an election to be an "S" corporation does not violate paragraph 4 of the Article. If a corporation elects to be an S corporation (requiring 35 or fewer shareholders), it is generally not subject to income tax and the shareholders take into account their pro rata shares of the corporation's items of income, loss, deduction or credit. (The purpose of the provision is to allow an individual or small group of individuals to conduct business in corporate form while paying taxes at individual rates as if the business were conducted directly.) A nonresident alien does not pay U.S. tax on a net basis, and, thus, does not generally take into account items of loss, deduction or credit. Thus, the S corporation provisions do not exclude corporations with nonresident alien shareholders because such shareholders are foreign, but only because they are not net-basis taxpayers. Similarly, the provisions exclude corporations with other types of shareholders where the purpose of the provisions cannot be fulfilled or their mechanics implemented. For example, corporations with corporate shareholders are excluded because the purpose of the provisions to permit individuals to conduct a business in corporate form at individual tax rates would not be furthered by their inclusion.

Paragraph 5

Paragraph 5 of the Article confirms that no provision of the Article will prevent either Contracting State from imposing the branch taxes described in Article 14 (Branch Tax). Since imposition of the branch taxes under the Convention is specifically sanctioned by Article 14, its imposition could not be precluded by Article 26, even without paragraph 5. Under the generally accepted rule of construction that the specific takes precedence over the more general, the specific branch tax provision of Article 14 would take precedence over the more general national treatment provision of Article 26.

Paragraph 6 of the U.S. Model provides nondiscrimination protection with respect to all taxes imposed by a Contracting State. Under this Article, nondiscrimination protection only applies to taxes covered by the Convention in Article 2 (Taxes Covered).

Relation to Other Articles

The saving clause of paragraph 2 of Article 1 (Personal Scope) does not apply to this Article, by virtue of the exceptions in paragraph 3(a) of Article 1. Thus, for example, a U.S. citizen who is a resident of Thailand may claim benefits in the United States under this Article.

Nationals of a Contracting State may claim the benefits of paragraph 1 regardless of whether they are entitled to benefits under Article 18 (Limitation on Benefits), because that paragraph applies to nationals and not residents. They may not claim the benefits of the other paragraphs of this Article with respect to an item of income unless they are generally entitled to treaty benefits with respect to that income under a provision of Article 18.

Article 27 (Mutual Agreement Procedure)

This Article provides the mechanism for taxpayers to bring to the attention of competent authorities issues and problems that may arise under the Convention. It also provides a mechanism for cooperation between the competent authorities of the Contracting States to resolve disputes and clarify issues that may arise under the Convention and to resolve cases of double taxation not provided for in the Convention. The competent authorities of the two Contracting States are identified in paragraph 1(e) of Article 3 (General Definitions).

Paragraph 1

Paragraph 1 provides that where a resident of a Contracting State considers that the actions of one or both Contracting States will result in taxation that is not in accordance with the Convention he may present his case to the competent authority of the Contracting State of which he is a resident or, if his case comes under paragraph 1 of Article 26 (Non-Discrimination), to the Contracting State of which he is a national.

Although the typical cases brought under this paragraph will involve economic double taxation arising from transfer pricing adjustments, the scope of this paragraph is not limited to such cases. For example, if a the United States treats income derived by a Thai company as attributable to a permanent establishment in the United States, and the Thai resident believes that the income is not attributable to a U.S. permanent establishment, the Thai resident may bring a complaint under paragraph 1 to the competent authority of Thailand.

It is not necessary for a person bringing a complaint first to have exhausted the remedies provided under the national laws of the Contracting States before presenting a case to the competent authorities. The case must be presented within three years of the first notification of the action resulting in taxation not in accordance with the Convention. Although the U.S. Model treaty would avoid any time limits for competent authority action, Thailand advocated a three-year limit, which is consistent with the OECD Model treaty.

Paragraph 2

Paragraph 2 instructs the competent authorities in dealing with cases brought by taxpayers under paragraph 1. It provides that if the competent authority of the Contracting State to which the case is presented judges the case to have merit, and cannot reach a unilateral solution, it shall seek an agreement with the competent authority of the other Contracting State pursuant to which taxation not in accordance with the Convention will be avoided. In a case where the taxpayer has entered a closing agreement (or other written settlement) with the United States prior to bringing a case to the competent authorities, the U.S. competent authority will endeavor only to obtain a correlative adjustment from Thailand. See, Rev. Proc. 96-13, 1996-1 C.B. 616, section 7.05.

Paragraph 3

Paragraph 3 authorizes the competent authorities to resolve difficulties or doubts that may arise as to the application or interpretation of the Convention. This Article follows the OECD Model treaty. The U.S. Model contains a non-exhaustive list of examples of the kinds of matters about which the competent authority may reach agreement. This list is not in the Convention. The U.S. Model list is merely illustrative, and is not intended to grant any authority that is not implicitly present as a result of the introductory sentence of paragraph 3. Thus, under this Article, the competent authorities may agree to settle a variety of conflicting applications of the Convention. The competent authorities may, for example, agree to the same attribution of income, deductions, credits or allowances between an enterprise in one Contracting State and its permanent establishment in the other or between related persons. These allocations are to be made in accordance with the arm's length principle underlying Article 7 (Business Profits) and Article 9 (Associated Enterprises). Agreements reached under these circumstances may include agreement on a methodology for determining an appropriate transfer price, common treatment of a taxpayer's cost sharing arrangement, or upon an acceptable range of results under that methodology. They may also agree to apply this methodology and range of results prospectively to future transactions and time periods pursuant to advance pricing agreements.

The competent authorities may also agree to characterize particular items of income in the same way, to characterize entities in a particular way, to apply the same source rules to particular items of income, and to adopt a common meaning of a term. The competent authorities can agree to the common application, consistent with the objective of avoiding double taxation, of procedural provisions of the internal laws of the Contracting States, including those regarding penalties, fines and interest. The competent authorities may seek agreement on a uniform set of standards for the use of exchange rates, or agree on consistent timing of gain recognition with respect to a transaction to the extent necessary to avoid double taxation.

Paragraph 3 explicitly authorizes the competent authorities to consult for the purpose of eliminating double taxation in cases not provided for in the Convention and to resolve any difficulties or doubts arising as to the interpretation or application of the Convention. This provision is intended to permit the competent authorities to implement the treaty in particular cases in a manner that is consistent with its expressed general purposes. It permits the competent authorities to deal with cases that are within the spirit of the provisions but that are not specifi-cally covered. An example of such a case might be double taxation arising from a transfer pricing adjustment between two permanent establishments of a third-country resident, one in the United States and one in Thailand. Since no resident of a Contracting State is involved in the case, the Convention does not apply, but the competent authorities nevertheless may use the authority of the Convention to prevent the double taxation.

Agreements reached by the competent authorities under paragraph 3 need not conform to the internal law provisions of either Contracting State. Paragraph 3 is not, however, intended to authorize the competent authorities to resolve problems of major policy significance that normally would be the subject of negotiations between the Contracting States themselves. For example, this provision would not authorize the competent authorities to agree to allow a U.S. foreign tax credit under the treaty for a tax imposed by the other country where that tax is not otherwise a covered tax and is not an identical or substantially similar tax imposed after the date of signature of the treaty. Whether or not the tax is creditable under the Code is a separate matter.

Paragraph 3 also authorizes the competent authorities to increase any dollar amounts referred to in the Convention to reflect economic and monetary developments. This refers to Article 15 (Independent Personal Services), Article 17 (Artistes and Sportsmen), and Article 22 (Students and Trainees). The rule under paragraph 4 is intended to operate as follows: if, for example, after the Convention has been in force for some time, inflation rates have been such as to make the threshold for entertainers unrealistically low in terms of the original objectives intended in setting the threshold, the competent authorities may agree to a higher threshold without the need for formal amendment to the treaty and ratification by the Contracting States. This authority can be exercised, however, only to the extent necessary to restore those original objectives. Because of paragraph 2 of Article 1 (General Scope), it is clear that this provision can be applied only to the benefit of taxpayers, i.e., only to increase thresholds, not to reduce them.

Paragraph 4

Paragraph 4 provides that if the competent authorities reach an agreement referred to in paragraphs 2 and 3, taxes shall be imposed on such income, and refund or credit of taxes shall be allowed by the Contracting States in accordance with such agreement. This is based on a provision in the Thailand-Finland treaty, and is similar to a provision in paragraph 2 of the U.S. Model treaty. Because, as specified in paragraph 4 of Article 1 (Personal Scope), the Convention cannot operate to increase a taxpayer's liability, time or other procedural limitations can be overridden only for the purpose of making refunds and not to impose additional tax.

Paragraph 5

Paragraph 5 provides that the competent authorities may communicate with each other for the purpose of reaching an agreement. This makes clear that the competent authorities of the two Contracting States may communicate without going through diplomatic channels. Such communication may be in various forms, including, where appropriate, through face-to-face meetings of representatives of the competent authorities.

<u>Other Issues</u>

Treaty effective dates and termination in relation to competent authority dispute resolution

A case may be raised by a taxpayer with respect to a year for which the Convention was in force after the Convention has been terminated. In such a case the ability of the competent authorities to act is limited. They may not exchange confidential information, nor may they reach a solution that varies from that specified in its law.

A case also may be brought to a competent authority under the Convention when it is in force, but with respect to a year prior to the entry into force. The scope of the competent authorities to address such a case is not constrained by the fact that the Convention was not in force when the transactions at issue occurred, and the competent authorities have available to them the full range of remedies afforded under this Article.

Triangular competent authority solutions

International tax cases may involve more than two taxing jurisdictions (<u>e.g.</u>, transactions among a parent corporation resident in a country A and its subsidiaries resident in countries B and C). As long as there is a complete network of treaties among the three countries, it should be possible, under the full combination of bilateral authorities, for the competent authorities of the three States to work together on a three-sided solution. Although Country A may not be able to give information received under Article 28 (Exchange of Information) from Country B to the authorities of country C, if the competent authorities of the three countries are working together, it should not be a problem for them to arrange for the authorities of Country B to give the necessary information directly to the tax authorities of country C, as well as to those of Country A. Each bilateral part of the trilateral solution must, of course, not exceed the scope of the authority of the competent authorities under the relevant bilateral treaty.

Relation to Other Articles

This Article is not subject to the saving clause of paragraph 2 of Article 1 (Personal Scope) by virtue of the exceptions in paragraph 3(a) of that Article. Thus, rules, definitions, procedures, etc. that are agreed upon by the competent authorities under this Article may be applied by the United States with respect to its citizens and residents even if they differ from the comparable Code provisions. Similarly, as indicated above, U.S. law may be overridden to provide refunds of tax to a U.S. citizen or resident under this Article. A person may seek relief under Article 27 regardless of whether he is generally entitled to benefits under Article 18 (Limitation on Benefits). As in all other cases, the competent authority is vested with the discretion to decide whether the claim for relief is justified.

Article 28 (Exchange of Information and Administrative Assistance)

Paragraph 1

This Article provides for the exchange of information between the competent authorities of the Contracting States. The information to be exchanged is that which is necessary for carrying out the provisions of the Convention or the domestic laws of the United States or of Thailand concerning the taxes covered by the Convention. Referring, as in the OECD Model, to information that is "necessary" for carrying out the provisions of the Convention is understood to be equivalent to the reference in the U.S. Model to information that is "relevant." Thus, use of the term "necessary" should not be interpreted as requiring a requesting State to demonstrate that it would be disabled from enforcing its tax laws unless it obtained a particular item of information.

The taxes covered by the Convention for purposes of this Article constitute a broader category of taxes than those referred to in Article 2 (Taxes Covered). As provided in paragraph 4, for purposes of exchange of information, covered taxes include all taxes imposed, in the case of the United States, under the Internal Revenue Code, and in the case of Thailand, under the Revenue Code and the Petroleum Income Tax Act. Exchange of information with respect to domestic law is authorized insofar as the taxation under those domestic laws is not contrary to the Convention. Thus, for example, information may be exchanged with respect to a covered tax, even if the transaction to which the information relates is a purely domestic transaction in the requesting State and, therefore, the exchange is not made for the purpose of carrying out the Convention.

An example of such a case is provided in the OECD Commentary: A company resident in the United States and a company resident in Thailand transact business between themselves through a third-country resident company. Neither Contracting State has a treaty with the third State. In order to enforce their internal laws with respect to transactions of their residents with the third-country company (since there is no relevant treaty in force), the Contracting State may exchange information regarding the prices that their residents paid in their transactions with the third-country resident.

Paragraph 1 states that information exchange is not restricted by Article 1 (General Scope). Accordingly, information may be requested and provided under this Article with respect to persons who are not residents of either Contracting State. For example, if a third-country resident has a permanent establishment in Thailand which engages in transactions with a U.S. enterprise, the United States could request information with respect to that permanent establishment, even though it is not a resident of either Contracting State. Similarly, if a third--country resident maintains a bank account in Thailand, and the Internal Revenue Service has reason to believe that funds in that account should have been reported for U.S. tax purposes but have not been so reported, information can be requested from Thailand with respect to that person's account.

Paragraph 1 also provides assurances that any information exchanged will be treated as secret, subject to the same disclosure constraints as information obtained under the laws of the requesting State. Information received may be disclosed only to persons, including courts and administrative bodies, concerned with the assessment, collection, enforcement or prosecution in respect of the taxes to which the information relates, or to persons concerned with the administration of these taxes. The information must be used by these persons in connection with these designated functions. Persons in the United States concerned with the administration of taxes include legislative bodies, such as the tax-writing committees of Congress and the General Accounting Office. Information received by these bodies must be for use in the performance of their role in overseeing the administration of U.S. tax laws. Information received may be disclosed in public court proceedings or in judicial decisions.

The Article authorizes the competent authorities to exchange information on a routine basis, on request in relation to a specific case, or spontaneously. It is contemplated that the Contracting States will utilize this authority to engage in all of these forms of information exchange, as appropriate.

Paragraph 2

Paragraph 2 is identical to paragraph 2 of Article 26 of the U.S. Model and paragraph 2 of Article 26 of the OECD Model. It provides that the obligations undertaken in paragraph 1 to exchange information do not require a Contracting State to carry out administrative measures that are at variance with the laws or administrative practice of either State. Nor is a Contracting State required to supply information not obtainable under the laws or administrative practice of either State, or to disclose trade secrets or other information, the disclosure of which would be contrary to public policy. Thus, a requesting State cannot obtain information from the other State if the information would be obtained pursuant to procedures or measures that are broader than those available in the requesting State.

While paragraph 2 states conditions under which a Contracting State is not obligated to comply with a request from the other Contracting State for information, the requested State is not precluded from providing such information, and may, at its discretion, do so subject to the limitations of its internal law.

Paragraph 3

Paragraph 3 provides that, subject to the provisions of paragraph 2 of Article 31 (Termination), when information is requested by a Contracting State in accordance with this Article, the other Contracting State is obligated to obtain the requested information as if the tax in question were the tax of the requested State, even if that State has no direct tax interest in the case to which the request relates.

The application of paragraph 3 is suspended until such time as the Government of the United States receives from the Government of Thailand a diplomatic note indicating that Thailand is prepared and able to implement the provisions of this paragraph. It is understood that Thailand will not be prepared and able to implement the provisions of this paragraph until enabling legislation has been enacted and has become effective. Paragraph 3 is subject to the provisions of paragraph 2 of Article 31 (Termination). Thus, the Convention shall terminate by operation of that paragraph on January 1 of the sixth year following its entry into force, unless the Government of the United States has received the diplomatic note described above from the Government of Thailand by June 30 of the fifth year following entry into force.

Paragraph 4

Notwithstanding the provisions of Article 2 (Taxes Covered), the exchange of information provided for in this Article shall apply to all taxes imposed by the United States under the Internal Revenue Code. In addition, the exchange of information provided for in this Article shall apply to all taxes imposed by Thailand under the Revenue Code, including the Petroleum Income Tax Act. The U.S. competent authority may, therefore, request information for purposes of, for example, estate and gift taxes or Federal excise taxes.

Treaty effective dates and termination in relation to competent authority dispute resolution

A tax administration may seek information with respect to a year for which the Convention was in force after the Convention has been terminated. In such a case the ability of the other tax administration to act is limited. The Convention no longer provides authority for the tax administrations to exchange confidential information. They may only exchange information pursuant to domestic law.

The competent authority also may seek information under the Convention at a time when the Convention is in force, but with respect to a year prior to the entry into force of the Convention. The scope of the competent authorities to address such a case is not constrained by the fact that the Convention was not in force when the transactions at issue occurred, and the competent authorities have available to them the full range of information exchange provisions afforded under this Article.

Article 29 (Diplomatic Agents and Consular Officers)

This Article confirms that any fiscal privileges to which diplomatic or consular officials are entitled under general provisions of international law or under special agreements will apply notwithstanding any provisions to the contrary in the Convention. The text of this Article is identical to the corresponding provision of the U.S. and OECD Models. The agreements referred to include any bilateral agreements, such as consular conventions, that affect the taxation of diplomats and consular officials and any multilateral agreements dealing with these issues, such as the Vienna Convention on Diplomatic Relations and the Vienna Convention on Consular Relations. The U.S. generally adheres to the latter because its terms are consistent with customary international law.

The Article does not independently provide any benefits to diplomatic agents and consular officers. Article 21 (Government Service) does so, as do Code section 893 and a number of bilateral and multilateral agreements. Rather, the Article specifically reconfirms in this context the statement in paragraph 4 of Article 1 (General Scope) that nothing in the tax treaty will operate to restrict any benefit accorded by the general rules of international law or with any other agreements referred to above. In the event that there is a conflict between the tax treaty and international law or such other treaties, under which the diplomatic agent or consular official is entitled to greater benefits under the latter, the latter laws or agreements shall have precedence. Conversely, if the tax treaty confers a greater benefit than another agreement, the affected person could claim the benefit of the tax treaty.

Pursuant to subparagraph 3(b) of Article 1, the saving clause of paragraph 2 of Article 1 (Personal Scope) does not apply to override any benefits of this Article available to an individual who is neither a citizen of the United States nor has immigrant status there.

Article 30 (Entry into Force)

This Article contains the rules for bringing the Convention into force and giving effect to its provisions.

Paragraph 1

Paragraph 1 provides for the ratification of the Convention by both Contracting States according to their constitutional and statutory requirements, and for the exchange of instruments of ratification at Washington, D.C.

In the United States, the process leading to ratification and entry into force is as follows: Once a treaty has been signed by authorized representatives of the two Contracting States, the Department of State sends the treaty to the President who formally transmits it to the Senate for its advice and consent to ratification, which requires approval by two-thirds of the Senators present and voting. Prior to this vote, however, it generally has been the practice for the Senate Committee on Foreign Relations to hold hearings on the treaty and make a recommendation regarding its approval to the full Senate. Both Government and private sector witnesses may testify at these hearings. After receiving the advice and consent of the Senate to ratification, the treaty is returned to the President for his signature on the ratification document. The President's signature on the document completes the process in the United States. When signed, it is ready for exchange.

Paragraph 2

Paragraph 2 provides that the Convention will enter into force upon the exchange of instruments of ratification. The date on which a treaty enters into force is not necessarily the date on which its provisions take effect. Paragraph 2, therefore, also contains rules that determine when the provisions of the treaty will have effect. Under paragraph 2(a), the Convention will have effect with respect to taxes withheld at source (principally dividends, interest and royalties) for amounts paid or credited on or after the first day of the sixth month following the date on which the Convention enters into force. For example, if instruments of ratification are exchanged on April 25 of a given year, the withholding rates specified in paragraph 2 of Article 10 (Dividends) would be applicable to any dividends paid or credited on or after October 1 of that year. This rule allows the benefits of the withholding reductions to be put into effect as soon as possible, without waiting until the following year. The delay of five to six months is required to allow sufficient time for withholding agents to be informed about the change in withholding rates.

For all other taxes, paragraph 2(b) specifies that the Convention will have effect for any taxable year or assessment period beginning on or after January 1 of the year next following entry into force.

As discussed under Articles 27 (Mutual Agreement Procedure) and 28 (Exchange of Information), the powers afforded the competent authority under these articles apply retroactively to taxable periods preceding entry into force.

Article 31 (Termination)

The Convention is to remain in effect indefinitely, unless terminated in accordance with the provisions of Article 31. The Convention may be terminated at any time after five years from the date in which the Convention enters into force, provided that at least six months notice is given through diplomatic channels. If notice of termination is given, the provisions of the Convention with respect to withholding at source will cease to have effect for amounts paid or credited on or after the first day of January next following the expiration of the six months period. For other taxes, the Convention will cease to have effect for taxable periods beginning on or after on the first day of January next following the expiration of the 6 months period.

Paragraph 1

A treaty performs certain specific and necessary functions regarding information exchange and mutual agreement. In the case of information exchange the treaty's function is to override confidentiality rules relating to taxpayer information. In the case of mutual agreement its function is to allow competent authorities to modify internal law in order to prevent double taxation and tax avoidance. With respect to the effective termination dates for these aspects of the treaty, therefore, if a treaty is terminated as of January 1 of a given year, no otherwise confidential information can be exchanged after that date, regardless of whether the treaty was in force for the taxable year to which the request relates. Similarly, no mutual agreement departing from internal law can be implemented after that date, regardless of the taxable year to which the agreement relates. Therefore, for the competent authorities to be allowed to exchange otherwise confidential information or to reach a mutual agreement that departs from internal law, a treaty must be in force at the time those actions are taken and any existing competent authority agreement ceases to apply.

Paragraph 1 of Article 29 relates only to unilateral termination of the Convention by a Contracting State. Nothing in that Article should be construed as preventing the Contracting States from concluding a new bilateral agreement, subject to ratification, that supersedes, amends or terminates provisions of the Convention without the six-month notification period.

Customary international law observed by the United States and other countries, as reflected in the Vienna Convention on Treaties, allows termination by one Contracting State at any time in the event of a "material breach" of the agreement by the other Contracting State.

Paragraph 2

Paragraph 2 is a sunset provision, made necessary because the application of paragraph 3 of Article 28 is suspended pending enactment of implementing legislation in Thailand. Under paragraph 2, the Convention will automatically terminate on January 1 of the sixth year following the year in which the Convention enters into force, unless the Government of the United States has received from the Government of Thailand by June 30 of the fifth year following entry into force a diplomatic note indicating that the Government of Thailand is prepared and able to implement the provisions of paragraph 3 of Article 28. Thus, the Convention will terminate, without the notification procedures of paragraph 1, unless the Government of Thailand indicates in a diplomatic note that if information is requested by the Government of United States, that the Government of Thailand is willing and able to obtain the requested information in the same manner and to the same extent as if the United States tax were being imposed by the Government of Thailand. If the Convention enters into force in 1997, the Convention will terminate on January 1, 2003 unless the diplomatic note is received by June 30, 2002.

Leopold
Wetland Management District

Comprehensive
Conservation Plan

Cover Photograph: U.S. Fish and Wildlife Service

The mission of the U.S. Fish & Wildlife Service is working with others to conserve, protect, and enhance fish and wildlife and their habitats for the continuing benefit of the American people.

The mission of the National Wildlife Refuge System is to administer a national network of lands and waters for the conservation, management and, where appropriate, restoration of the fish, wildlife and plant resources and their habitats within the United States for the benefit of present and future generations of Americans.

Comprehensive Conservation Plans provide long-term guidance for management decisions; set forth goals, objectives and strategies needed to accomplish refuge purposes; and, identify the Fish and Wildlife Service's best estimate of future needs. These plans detail program planning levels that are sometimes substantially above current budget allocations and, as such, are primarily for Service strategic planning and program prioritization purposes. The plans do not constitute a commitment for staffing increases, operational and maintenance increases, or funding for future land acquisition.

Leopold

Wetland Management District

Comprehensive Conservation Plan Approval

Submitted by:

Steven J. Lenz   _Sept. 17, 2008_

Steven J. Lenz   Date
District Manager

Concur:

James T. Leach   _9-23-08_

James T. Leach   Date
Refuge Supervisor, Area 3

Nita M. Fuller   _9.25.2008_

Nita M. Fuller   Date
Regional Chief, National Wildlife Refuge System

Approve:

Charlie Wooley   _9/25/08_

Robyn Thorson   Date
Regional Director

Charles M. Wooley
Acting Regional Director